MW00463720

WHAT'S
WRONG
with me?

A girl's book
of lessons learned,
inspiration and
advice

DAREE ALLEN

KHARACTER DISTINCTION BOOKS
ATLANTA, GEORGIA

Scriptures taken from the Holy Bible, New International Version, NIV. Copyright © 1973, 1978, 1984, 2011 by Biblica, Inc. Used by permission of Zondervan. All rights reserved worldwide. **www.zondervan.com**.

Scripture quotations taken from AMPLIFIED BIBLE, Copyright © 1954, 1958, 1962, 1964, 1965, 1987 by The Lockman Foundation. All rights reserved. Used by permission. (**www.Lockman.org**)

Scripture taken from THE MESSAGE. Copyright © 1993, 1994, 1995, 1996, 2000, 2001, 2002. Used by permission of NavPress Publishing Group.

Scripture quotations marked (CEV) are from the Contemporary English Version Copyright © 1991, 1992, 1995 by American Bible Society, Used by Permission.

Scripture quotations marked "NKJV™" are taken from the New King James Version. Copyright © 1982 by Thomas Nelson, Inc. Used by permission. All rights reserved.

Scripture quotations marked NLT are taken from the *Holy Bible,* New Living Translation, copyright © 1996, 2004, 2007 by Tyndale House Foundation. Used by permission of Tyndale House Publishers, Inc., Carol Stream, Illinois 60188. All rights reserved.

Kharacter Distinction Books
4355 Cobb Parkway
Suite J185
Atlanta, GA 30339
Printed in the United States of America
Copyright © 2012 by Daree Allen

Design and Composition: LeftRight Collaborative
Design: Jennifer Rogers Tyson, www.leftrightcollaborative.com
Design Revisions: Mélissa Caron, Enki Communications, www.go-enki.com
Author Photo Credit: Innovation Photography, www.InnovationPics.com

All rights reserved. No part of this publication may be reproduced, stored in a retrieval system, or transmitted by any means—electronic, mechanical, photographic (photocopying), recording, or otherwise—without prior permission in writing from the publisher, except by a reviewer, who may quote brief passages in a review.

What's Wrong With Me? is a work of nonfiction, but the author has changed the names of the people depicted in the stories herein.

This book contains information gathered from many sources and personal experiences. It is published and sold with the understanding that neither the author nor the publisher is rendering any legal, accounting, or psychological advice. The author and the publisher disclaim any personal liability for the advice and information presented herein. Although the author and the publisher have prepared this manuscript with diligence, careful to ensure the accuracy of the information presented, they assume no responsibility for errors, inaccuracies, omissions, or inconsistencies herein.

ISBN: 978-0-9837455-0-1
LCCN: 2011911385

praise for
WHAT'S WRONG WITH ME?

"What's Wrong with Me takes the reader on a poignant journey of self-discovery by identifying the complex mix of psychological, environmental, spiritual, and socio-cultural influences that can help young women move towards positive and progressive lives that are guided by catalysts of empowerment, resilience and healing."

DR. KISHA B. HOLDEN, PhD
ASSOCIATE PROFESSOR OF CLINICAL PSYCHIATRY,
MOREHOUSE SCHOOL OF MEDICINE

"I wish this book was available for me and my friends when we were teenagers. It is *that* powerful. It gives helpful, spiritual guidance to young girls, touching on every aspect of their lives... from dating to dieting to deliverance... it's all here. Whether she's struggling with relationships, single motherhood inadequacies, money woes or her own self-worth, *What's Wrong With Me* will help the young teen sort through her thoughts and place her on the path to self-assuredness."

MONTRIE RUCKER ADAMS
APR, CHIEF VISIBILITY OFFICER, VISIBILITY MARKETING INC.

"Dynamic author Daree Allen dares to go there with teens in her inspiring piece *"What's Wrong With Me?"* She does parents and educators a favor by opening a dialogue on the universal challenges that young girls will often secretly face that can ultimately build or destroy dreams. Pick up a copy of this book and arm a young lady with the key that unlocks a successful life."

RAE PEARSON BENN
AUTHOR OF *STILL STANDING*, INFINITY PUBLISHING, 2005

dedication

I dedicate this book to my daughter Kaia. May she know her value, her beauty, and her strength early—and not learn it the hard way.

I also dedicate this book to my maternal great-grandmother, Alzadie Turner, whom I never knew. She died before I was born, but I've heard so many wonderful things about her loving nature.

This book is for all the teen girls out there who are trying to find their own voice. Also, it's for those without healthy, positive role models, for those who want better for themselves, those who know God put them here for a great purpose, and for those who are still searching for their purpose.

For the girls who don't like themselves, wish they were smarter, prettier, had a family with more money, or a parent like someone else's. I've been that girl.

For the girls who can't wait to get out of their parents' house so they can do whatever they want, whenever they want. I've been that girl, too.

For those who sometimes feel like they want to give up, but there's something inside that keeps them pushing forward to something better. I'm still that girl (sometimes).

This book is for all of you.

"All praise to God, the Father of our Lord Jesus Christ.
God is our merciful Father and the source of all comfort.
He comforts us in all our troubles so that we can
comfort others. When they are troubled, we will be able
to give them the same comfort God has given us."
(1 Corinthians 1:3-4 NIV)

contents

CONTENTS

CONTENTS

introduction

LESSONS LEARNED

Our beliefs are manifested in our actions. Everything we do is rooted in our thinking. If you think about something long enough—good or bad—you'll act on it.

What do you think about yourself? Your looks? Your potential? Your family and friends? Are you hopeful or hopeless? Jaded or optimistic? Feel like giving up, but something deep inside tells you you're worth more than all *that*? It may come as no surprise, then, to hear how God instilled a truth and a purpose in every one of us. We can make better decisions in our lives if we just think about that purpose *differently*.

In fact, if positive thinking leads to positive acting, the result can be "glorious living," according to Scripture:

> *"It's in Christ that we find out who we are and what we are living for. Long before we first heard of Christ and got our hopes up, he had his eye on us, had designs on us for glorious living, part of the overall purpose he is working out in everything and everyone."*
> **(Ephesians 1:11-12 *The Message*)**

When I look back, I wish I had a different mindset, because I would not only have acted differently, but would have made better decisions.

I always loved music and my family, and wanted to be good-looking and accepted by my peers. I wanted to be asked out on dates, and to be called by girls who wanted to do more than just chat—but also to be my friend. I didn't have a boyfriend until I was 17 and out of high school. This was the same person I lost my virginity to; the experience taught me a lot of hard lessons that some of my friends learned much earlier—some of which I will share with you throughout this book.

I never had a big sister, a "Big Mama"-like figure or "auntie," or a mentor to teach me how to become a young lady and give me advice. I just looked to my peers, who I now realize were just trying to make it, like I was. That mentor figure has always been missing in my life. If this situation sounds familiar, I'd like to be a positive mentor or role model for you.

WHAT YOU'LL FIND INSIDE...

I wrote this book because I want you—as teens and young women—to avoid potential pitfalls as you embark on the adventure part of growing up and "coming of age." I've always known I was destined to be successful in life, but I encountered many distractions on my journey that could have altered this course. No matter where you are today, it's not good enough to simply get through your situation—you must *overcome* it and draw strength from lessons learned along the way.

There are many empowering messages I want you to get from this book. Some situations aren't discussed in this book because I haven't experienced them, such as abortion, rape or molestation, death of a close friend, or blended families.

Topics I *will* cover about in this book include:
- Not fitting in with others
- Friendships
- Premarital sex and teen pregnancy
- Self-esteem and acceptance
- Domestic violence
- How God sees us
- What God expects from us

Each chapter concludes with a section entitled "Consider This," which has some thoughts and points for you to reflect on and remember. Think of it as a quick reference to the overarching messages in the chapter. It is followed by a list of books related to the chapter's topic, "Further Reading." Use these resources for additional insight and depth into the information we'll cover together in this book.

"WHAT'S WRONG WITH ME?"

You may have asked yourself this question many times, in many situations. Throughout this book, my aim is to convince you that although we all have moments of confusion, frustration and self-doubt, *nothing* is wrong with you.

As an overview, here are six truths you should know up front. These are things I wish I had known, believed, and acted on when *I* was a girl.

1. *You are loved.* If by no one else but God, that's more than enough. You should love yourself unconditionally before you love others. You don't need acceptance, admiration, adoration, or affection from anyone to define you or give you self-worth. God has given you everything you need (gifts, talents, resources, friends, mentors) to find your way!

2. *You're beautiful just the way you are.* We all have imperfections, but God doesn't make mistakes.

3. *When you get older and look back, you'll see* it *"wasn't all that."* When I was a teen, many of the people I used to look up to or thought were more likable, prettier, or more popular than I was did not maintain those positions as adults. Back in the day, I cared about who was going with whom, who was friends with whom, and—later—who was having sex with whom. Trust me, no matter how important it seems to you now, it's not going to matter for long.

4. *Be independent.* You don't have to rely on a guy or anyone else for money, or to determine your self-worth, security, or value. You can secure your own bank account, car, and home, and experience what it's like to live on your own before settling down, getting married, and raising a family. (I know it doesn't always happen in this order, but work with me.)

5. *Never settle.* You can work for—and wait for—the best life has to offer. Set goals—you'll achieve them if you stick with it. In the meantime, don't be afraid to enjoy your singleness. Be content with where you are in life, whether it's your relationship status, career, or anything else you're working on. You never know how long (or short) each season of your life will last.

6. *Make a conscious decision to do what's right, instead of what's easy.* Don't give up and in due time you will reap the harvest of what you've sown.

Even now, I still sometimes have to remind myself of these truths. I haven't totally mastered them all. I have to encourage myself to keep moving forward, praying, and believing in God and myself. I want the best for me and for you, and so does He.

part one

MY PERSONAL LIFE—ME, MYSELF & I

WHAT'S **WRONG** with who I am?

> *"The value of identity, of course,*
> *is that so often with it comes purpose."*
> — **RICHARD GRANT** —

Have you ever heard someone say they're "trying to find themselves"? An identity crisis can occur at any age and at various times throughout one's life. The age doesn't matter; it's what you do with this experience and how you let it shape you that matters.

In this chapter, you will get to know me a little bit, and you may see some similarities to yourself or ideas you have about yourself.

MATCH GAME

As I was growing up, various things made me stand out. My appearance, for one.

My sister and I were an early version of the R&B super group, Destiny's Child—at least in terms of our clothes. The group members always wore matching outfits, made by Beyoncé's mother, Tina Knowles. My mom did the same thing with my sister and I in the '80s, even though we weren't a singing group (and in my mom's case, she was probably channeling The Supremes). But my mom made most of the clothes my sister and I wore when we were little, and on Sundays, my sister and I would go to church in matching outfits. They weren't exactly the same, but as Tina did, my mom used similar matching pieces, and she made them age-appropriate. My sister is five years younger than I, so her dresses were very frilly and cute. I've never been big on wearing dresses, or dressing up, period, but I was at the mercy of my mother when it came to my hair and wardrobe. If she liked it, that's was what I was stuck with.

I remember being teased about my clothes during elementary school. Most of the time, the other kids would be in awe that my mother sewed my clothes instead of buying my entire wardrobe at Sears or some other department store. One day a girl asked me if my mother made my bra and panties, too, and the other kids laughed. (In case you're wondering, she didn't.)

THE GEEK SHALL INHERIT THE EARTH

I was a nerd—at least to some extent. Sometimes the other kids made fun of me because I did my homework every day, and I enunciated my words (some people call this "talking proper"). Wearing not-so-stylish glasses didn't help, either. I was a bookworm, too. I read hundreds (yes, literally hundreds) of books as a girl. I loved going to the school library every few days for new books. Unfortunately, as I became a teenager, I hated being seen as smart, because to me, smart did not equal popular. Sometimes I would "dumb down" to fit in with some of the popular kids I admired, acting like I knew less than I did, and skipping classes. I was known as the smart girl who did her homework, knew the answers in class, and wore glasses, so I was not the girl who got asked out by boys or invited to popular girls' homes to hang out. I was ashamed of being smart because it interfered with my perceptions of my attractiveness. Little did I know that all these differences would set me up and prepare me to be a better-adjusted, responsible person. You shouldn't have to change who you are to be liked by others. But back then, it was all about social conformity and "fitting in."

> **I was ashamed of being smart because it interfered with my perceptions of my attractiveness.**

"WHERE YOU FROM?"

I grew up in upstate New York, but I left in my early 20's. Ever since then, when people hear the way I talk, they ask where I'm from. I usually don't answer with "Utica, New York," because I don't feel like trying to explain where it is and answer more questions. If I just say "New York," they automatically think I mean New York City, but they'll still ask, "What part?," so I try to keep it short and sweet by answering, "I'm from upstate New York." This answer can also be a problem, since 'upstate' is a relative term. Some people consider White Plains or Yonkers to be upstate—it depends on where you live. I always hope that adding the word "upstate" will let people know that I'm not claiming any of the New York City boroughs as my home, but some people are just curious, and that answer doesn't always satisfy them, so the next probing question is...

"What part?"

"Utica."

Silence.

"It's about 45 minutes from Syracuse."

"Oh, OK" they say, and you can see they have a real point of reference.

Everyone sees something different when they look at you. We all make our own judgments, even if only subconsciously. It's human nature. And some people want to see if they can size you up or figure you out right off the bat, so they can put you in a category or stereotype you based on how they perceive you. Comments like, "You know how you New Yorkers are," "Y'all don't know how to drive," or something derogatory about "women from New York" are all par for the course. I do my best to resist the urge to tell them off because then they'll continue to think New Yorkers are mean. Oh, yeah, and then there's my favorite: "You don't have a New York accent, and I can tell you're not from here, either." I feel like saying, 'OK, so what? I don't have to prove anything to you,' but I don't.

Along with trying to figure out my "accent" come the comments about my diction and enunciation when I speak, such as "You speak so proper," or "You sound like a White girl." Since when are all Whites intelligent and able to speak English better than Blacks? Black people need to know how to use the English language, too, right?

I realize I should ignore ignorant comments like these instead of getting offended or reacting to them, but even in my 30s, I still encounter variations of these types of comments from young and old alike because of their pervasive (but incorrect) perceptions of how I should sound when I talk. Is it really that big a deal? I can brush it off now, but it used to get to me.

If my identity isn't tested because of my voice or where I'm from, then it's my looks. (More on that in the next chapter.)

WHO YOU ARE

One day in my freshman year of college, I was talking to my roommate, and I made this statement: "I know who I am, and that's more important than what I am." It's a good affirmation. You have to get to know who you are, be assertive, secure in it, and unashamed of it.

If you don't know who you are, it's easy to get sucked into other people's ideas of who you should be, and you can easily become vulnerable to other people's demands and desires. Your parents or friends may have ideas on the career you should pursue, the kind of life you should lead, and the types of activities you should get into, but you have to decide what you want to do. It's OK to be alone sometimes to find out what you like to do and discover the things that interest you and make you feel good. You don't have to be with your best friend or boyfriend every waking moment. You can take career or personal interest inventories to assess your skills and find a job or career that you may find fulfilling, which we'll discuss later. But it all starts with tuning in to yourself—then you can discover your purpose and develop goals around that through prayer, coaching, and staying aware of your surroundings and opportunities that come along.

CONSIDER THIS

God knows us because He made us in His own image. It's easy to get caught up in what celebrities and your friends are doing, and keeping up with the popular kids at school. But don't get lost in all of that. Go back to the basics, back to the Word of God (the Bible) to discover who you are, your talents, and gifts. Don't look to others for constant confirmation, or develop approval addiction. It's a surefire way to lose yourself. We'll talk about this more in Chapter 6, "What's Wrong With My Friends?"

FURTHER READING

Learning who you are and finding yourself will take time. While you reflect, check out some tips from the book *Be U: Be Honest, Be Beautiful, Be Intentional, Be Strong, Be You!* by the contemporary gospel duo Mary Mary. And after that, marvel at the self-doubt and hurt that the iconic superstar Janet Jackson overcame as shared in her memoir, *True You: A Journey to Finding and Loving Yourself.*

2

WHAT'S **WRONG** with my looks?

"People are like stained glass windows:
They sparkle and shine when the sun is out,
but when the darkness sets in their true beauty
is revealed only if there is a light within."

— **ELIZABETH KUBLER-ROSS** —

---

*A*s females, it seems like we always want something someone else has without appreciating what we do have. If we have straight hair, we wish it was curlier. If we have fine hair, we wish it was thicker. Some of us with a curvy shape wish we were thinner, and those of us who are short wish we were taller. Bigger/smaller nose, breasts, legs, or booty—it's hard for us to accept ourselves as is—or feel like we're "just right."

October 8, 1990, 10:13 p.m.
Lord, when are my boobs gonna grow some more?
Why do I have to be flat-chested? I'll bet any
amount of money that my sister's hooters are
bigger than mine by the time she's 21...

I was right—and it didn't take that long.

I didn't like my looks as a teen, either. I wore bangs for years because I had a lot of pimples on my forehead, and also had them on my back. I had a light moustache that was just dark enough so you could see it. I was unhappy with my small breasts, and sometimes I was teased because of my hair, which is very thick, coarse, and bushy—unlike my mother and sister. I didn't start wearing a relaxer in my hair until I was in high school, and my mother didn't know how to handle it in its natural state other than to press it with a hot comb (no flat irons back then) or braid it.

My body is pear-shaped, which I inherited from my Gramma. My top half is much smaller than my wide hips, thick thighs, and big booty. I noticed my shape around sixth grade, and so did everyone else. One of those memorable times was on the first day of junior high school (seventh grade).

I began seventh grade in a new school with all eyes on me. I found a black catsuit two weeks before school started, during our family summer vacation in Boston. Oddly enough, when I tried it on in Filene's Basement, my mother and her friend approved of the outfit. Thinking back, it did look good on me, but it caused quite a stir at school, and I got a lot of attention and compliments from both boys and girls. When I think about it now, I consider that outfit to be inappropriate for a 13-year-old to wear to school. People still remember that catsuit and ask me about it to this day!

But I didn't always feel confident in form-fitting clothes. It takes most of us years before we totally accept our bodies as they are—if ever—and I am no different. I had a phase where I used to hide my body by putting on long shirts that covered my butt. Some girls wear big clothes to cover up their shape; others wear clothes that are too tight to flaunt their shape. Both are wrong. Big clothes only make you look bigger (if you don't believe me, watch a couple of episodes of *What Not to Wear* on the The Learning Channel, where clueless fashion misfits get schooled). You can wear what fits you and still be classy. More on this in a minute.

Now my attitude is different. So what if my breasts are small and my butt is big? Does the size of either make me smarter or dumber? No. Do they attract or distract guys, making us females more or less desirable? Maybe, but who cares? The male species is attracted to a wide variety of body types, and it started long before Sir Mix-a-Lot's most popular song, "Baby Got Back," and well before the likes of Beyoncé, Serena Williams, Jennifer Lopez and Kim Kardashian came on the scene flaunting their curvy behinds.

DON'T BELIEVE THE (MEDIA) HYPE

Celebrities, models, and other stars you see on TV, in music videos, movies and magazines all have to spend hours upon hours getting glammed up. They have personal trainers, chefs, stylists, make-up artists, and beauticians working together to create the ultimate finished image for the camera. If you had a glam squad hooking you up for a few hours, you would look like that, too. Not to mention the photo retouching and airbrushing.

Shaun Robinson, an anchor on "Access Hollywood" and author of a book I highly recommend you read, *Exactly as I Am*, visited Oprah's all-girl school in Africa and noted how the girls' lack of exposure to the media allowed them to develop confidence without those distractions.[1] I think we would be better off, too, by limiting our daily media intake.

You can be beautiful no matter what size or shape you are. In Tyra Banks' 2007 "So What!" campaign, she promoted healthy body image and encouraged young women everywhere to embrace the flaws all of us have—even this world-renowned-former-supermodel-turned-talk-show host!

GOOD AND BAD HAIR DAYS

Ahhh, bad hair days. I've had more than my fair share of them. My mother and sister have soft, wavy hair that's easy to manipulate—nothing like mine. My mother didn't hide her frustration when it was time to press my hair or braid it after I washed it. My mom found my hair hard to manage, especially when I got to the age where I no longer wore cornrows and little-girl plaits. But I loved to get my hair "done"—it made me feel so good. To me, getting my hair done was the best feeling in the world, and an instant confidence-booster when I came out of the salon looking fly. And the whole ordeal of getting my hair "done" every few weeks, sitting in salons for hours, subjecting my scalp to burns from the lye (sodium hydroxide) in the perm and excessive heat from the hair dryers—it was all heavily rooted in wanting to achieve styles and a hair texture that made me feel better about myself—again, wanting what I didn't have. So whether I had a Jheri-curl, a perm, or box braid extensions, I felt like I was at my best when my hair was on point. I used to cut pictures out of magazines like *Hype Hair, Sophisticate's Black Hair, Ebony*, and *Essence* that I wanted to emulate, but I could never reproduce my stylist's work at home the next day. (NOTE: I don't know why Blacks and Whites use the term "perm" differently: I use it to refer to a chemical process that permanently straightens the hair, while Whites refer to perms as chemical process that permanently curls the hair).

I remember one day at school when I was about 15, and at lunch, one of my friends noticed that I had a big patch of hair missing from the side of my head! I don't know how I hadn't noticed, but it definitely happened during my weekend visit to a local beauty school. (It wasn't my first or last visit, as my funds were limited, but thank God that never happened again!)

September 24, 1991, 5:10 p.m.
My hair determines my self-esteem. If I like
my hairstyle, I like myself, and vice versa.

The notion of having a bad hair day was very real to me, but I took it to the extreme: My self-esteem was wrapped up in my hair. Believe it or not, millions of grown women still feel this way.

Consider the 2009 documentary, *Good Hair,* which explored Black womens' obsession with their hair, causing them to spend thousands of dollars on hair weaves and relaxers, a.k.a., the "creamy crack." I don't know who taught us to hate our natural hair. Whatever the reason, hair care is a billion-dollar industry, and Black women are a large part of that.

In 2010, after relaxing my hair for 20 years (at 4- to 6-week intervals), I started looking into what it would take for me to start wearing my hair natural again. I wasn't in a rush, but I began reading blogs and watching YouTube videos that answered questions about styling and maintaining natural hair. After all, you don't see many White women trying to make their hair look like ours—they embrace their texture. Why couldn't I?

Not only that, but my daughter was asking me questions about why she couldn't wear her hair down like the other little girls at school. When I came home from the salon with my hair flat ironed or with a Dominican blow-out, it was straight and silky, falling past my shoulders. She loved the look and wanted me to do the same thing to her hair. I didn't want her to think that her hair has to be straight or swing to be beautiful, so I examined my own beliefs about my hair, did some research, and then did the big chop. I didn't think I could deal with styling my natural hair, but I remembered when I first learned how to roll my hair with rollers, use a curling iron, and so on, and I knew after an adjustment, I'd be alright.

These days I've learned that although I still allow my hair's "behavior" to affect my mood, good hair is simply healthy hair—straight or curly, kinky (not nappy—sounds too negative) or smooth, light or dark. It's all about you feeling comfortable with yourself (not your peers, co-workers, or family members), and looking your best. You represent you all day, so do it right!

CHECK YOURSELF AT THE DOOR

This goes for your wardrobe as well. No one should care more about your appearance—or what you're wearing—than you. That means no matter what size you are—4 to 24—you should wear clothes that fit you, look good on you, and make you feel confident. More and more clothes are being made to accommodate all kinds of sizes and shapes. But I shake my head sometimes when I see how some people wear jeans that don't cover their behinds, or shirts that don't cover their bellies. Take a little pride in yourself by acknowledging some basic principles of dressing excellence.

**You can look good
no matter what size you are.**

Your shirt is too small if:

- The buttons are holding on for dear life, pulling the sides of your shirt so far apart you can see "O's" down the front of your blouse, not to mention your bra underneath.
- You can see the skin on the bottom of your stomach. Not cute. If you have rolls or a "pooch," don't accentuate it with a tight shirt.
- The armholes are rolled up in your armpits, and we can't see the entire hem of your sleeves.

Your pants/jeans don't fit if:

- You can see your ankles while you're standing up (which means your pants are too short).
- Anyone can see your crack when you're standing or bent over. Either your pants are too small, or you may need a higher rise.
- If you have to lie on your bed, jump up and down, or hold in your gut to zip up your pants.

Your undergarments don't fit right if:

- Your bra creates breast bubbles under your shirt. In that case, your bra is too small, and you probably need to go up a cup size (get a proper bra fitting in a department store).
- You can see your bra or panty lines through the clothing—that's what Spanx and other shapers are for. They smooth rolls, lift breasts, and eliminate panty lines. Try one on, and you can see the difference instantly!

In general, your rule of thumb should be: if you have to squeeze into it, it doesn't fit!

Love It or Leave It

If you own any clothing that violates the preceding principles, say your goodbyes—but keep the memories (take a pic if you want to)—and let the clothes go. Don't torture them or yourself another day. Put them in a big bag, and drop them off at your local Salvation Army or other charity of choice. Sharing is caring.

For a thorough reality check on your clothing, do the "love it or leave it" inventory and ask yourself the following four questions about each article of clothing in your closet. It's easy to get overwhelmed with this task, so you may want to take a few days, depending on the size of your wardrobe, and/or enlist the help of an honest, no-nonsense friend to get it done in one shot (why risk the temptation to keep hoarding or prolong the pain?).

ASK YOURSELF:	IF...	THEN...
1. Do I still like this item?	Yes >	Proceed to the next question.
	No >	Donate it to charity or a friend who wants it.*
2. Does this item still fit me? *(Keep it real—refer back to "Check Yourself at the Door," refer back to the section "Check Yourself at the Door.")*	Yes >	Proceed to the next question.
	No >	Donate it to charity or a friend who wants it.*
3. Do I receive compliments when I wear this item? Does this item make me feel good when I put it on? Is it comfortable and does it suit my body?	Yes > (to all)	Proceed to the next question.
	No > (to some or all)	Donate it to charity or a friend who wants it.*
4. Have I worn this item in the past year? Will it be in style next year? *(NOTE: If you have nothing to coordinate it with, hold it in a separate "maybe" pile. Then once you finish with all the items in your closet, go back through the "maybe" pile and decide whether to donate it or make a match).*	Yes > (to all)	Proceed to the next question.
	No > (to some or all)	Donate it to charity or a friend who wants it.*

* When it comes to a clothing swap, please note, do not pass on a dud! If you really care about your friends, don't offer them something that doesn't fit them or is otherwise unflattering.

You can learn a lot about how to dress by watching *What Not to Wear* on The Learning Channel (TLC)—I did. The show helped me understand how to dress for my body type and how to find clothes that fit and pair them with clothes I already own.

Not only is it important to know what to wear but also what not to wear and when to part with clothing that's not right for you (see "Love It or Leave It," below). Your image really suffers when you wear clothes that don't fit. Like it or not, we judge people based on how they look—partly because if we don't know someone, we have to start somewhere, and it usually starts with first impressions.

In case you think I'm contradicting myself, let me be clear. I'm not talking about trying to portray a false image to impress people; I'm talking about representing the best you. Some situations this is especially called for are job interviews, meeting new people, and first dates. In these instances, you will be judged by the way you look, but wearing clothes that help you feel confident and show off your best features tastefully will work in your favor.

IT ALL STARTS WITH YOU

It's normal to wish that you looked differently sometimes, but realize your value is ultimately based on what's inside, despite what anyone says. You have to start with you. What kind of self-talk goes on in your head? What kinds of things do you say to yourself day after day?

There's no one else like you! Have you accepted yourself for the wonderful, unique person you are? If not, you have to make peace with your identity and how you look physically. While you're sitting around wishing that you had a nose like your friend's, hair like your neighbor's, legs like your cousin's, or hair like your sister's, those people are likely quietly wishing they were like you in some way, too—it's true! We're all different, and everyone has something to be admired for—including you.

There's nothing wrong with admiring someone, but you have to be careful not to put yourself down when you do it. Saying things like: "I wish I looked like her" is negative self-talk. As it's clearly stated in Psalm 139:14, "You are fearfully and wonderfully made" (NIV). What a great affirmation, straight from the Creator Himself! God doesn't make mistakes. He knew you before He created the earth, and He created you, too.

CONSIDER THIS

Comparing yourself to other girls is normal—everyone admires something about someone else's appearance—but don't stress about it. And by all means don't focus on Hollywood celebrities (who have trainers, cooks, and make-up artists at their beck and call). They have an image to uphold, and it's not based on reality. After all, the average American woman wears a size 14.

More than anyone's approval, you have to love yourself. If you don't like what's in the mirror, what can you do to change it? Is it even in your power to change it? The solution probably doesn't lie in make-up or plastic surgery. When it comes to your physical looks that you can't change, the answer lies in acceptance. Many times, life presents challenges to you, and you'll find that there are some things you'll have to accept as is. If you don't accept your looks now, you risk a life of discontentment and misery, because without acceptance, there's nothing else you can do but get frustrated.

Remember, how you feel about yourself is all in your attitude. Do you spend a lot of time with negative people who put you down or tease you because of your looks? People like this are toxic, and people that are toxic kill your self-esteem if you spend too much time around them. Try to limit or eliminate these influences from your life as much as possible. I'll talk about this more in the next chapter, *"What's Wrong With the Way I Feel?"*

FURTHER READING

Clueless about picking out clothes or overall fashion for your body type? Study *Oh No, She Didn't!: The Top 100 Style Mistakes and How to Avoid Them* by Clinton Kelly and *Dress Your Best: The Complete Guide to Finding the Style That's Right for Your Body* by Clinton Kelly and Stacy London.

WHAT'S **WRONG** with the way I feel?

*"It's not who you are that holds you back,
it's who you think you're not."*

— **AUTHOR UNKOWN** —

*T*he average person has about 60,000 thoughts per day. According to scientists, roughly 45,000 of those thoughts tend to be negative.[2] I think for most of my life, that number has been a lot higher.

Everyone has feelings, and no matter how strong they are, the challenge is not to overreact to them in the heat of the moment—whether they're feelings of sexual temptation, hopelessness, or anger.

It's no secret I have a temper. I used to have temper tantrums as a child, and sometimes I would slam doors when I got mad. Other times, I could slip into depression for the same reasons that I would have the tantrum—because of hopelessness or feeling out of control. Not having a say in certain aspects of my life made me feel lost and helpless. I also didn't accept myself or have much self-love.

October 4, 1990, 10:25 p.m.

I wish I could die now. Really. Like in my sleep.
To put me out of my misery. I don't feel ANYWHERE
close to adults, God, Deanna, or any of my so-called
family and friends. Let me explain to you why:

———

My family only sees the exterior.
They don't really know me.

———

I can't name one person I could call
a true friend of mine.

———

God? It's too complicated to begin with.

———

Adults have their own petty worries and concerns.

———

If I died right now, who would come to my funeral?
Who would cry over me? Who would be happy?
I will ALWAYS wonder about that.

———

I am in pain, and no one gives a damn, really.
I'm pretty sure nothing would change without me.
Who the hell loves me and how can they prove it?

MIND GAMES

At one time or another, we've said or heard someone exclaim, "What was he thinking?" Our behavior starts in our mind. Pastor, speaker, and author Dr. Creflo A. Dollar, who has written books that some Christian colleges use for their curricula, illustrates how important words and thoughts are with this chain:

———

Words become thoughts; thoughts become feelings;
feelings become decisions, decisions become actions,
actions become habits, habits become character,
and character becomes destiny.

Dollar says that if you don't like where you are, change the previous link in the chain. It's true. So much of what we feel, think, and say is reflected in our behavior, which in turn affects our future. We can impact our destiny years before it comes to pass!

When someone tries to insult you by calling you names or "talks down" to you in a disrespectful tone, you recognize it pretty quickly. But what about the negative self-talk that goes on in your mind? Sometimes we can be harder on ourselves than our enemies are.

What's going on in your head? What are you feeding your mind? Do you listen to music, read books, or watch TV shows and movies that lead to feelings of discontentment with your life? What you feed your mind can lead to negative self-talk—that is, saying things to yourself (or having thoughts) like: "I'm so stupid," "I'm afraid to do that," or "I'll never be as good at that as he/she is."

The command to "Love your neighbor as yourself" implies that you love yourself (see Mark 12:31). And when you love yourself, you have a good sense of self-esteem, and you won't disrespect yourself by thinking or saying negative things about yourself. Remember, words become thoughts, and from there, those negative or positive thoughts will manifest in turn.

But what if you don't know how to stop yourself from thinking negative thoughts about yourself or others? Try identifying those thoughts that come to you over and over again when you get frustrated or upset. Then take them one by one and replace them with good thoughts, which come from speaking a positive affirmation. The positive affirmation can come from a promise in the Bible, or from simply flipping the negative thought to its opposite. Here's a simple example:

Let's say you leave for school one morning, and something goes wrong unexpectedly (you forgot your oral report note cards at home, you left your purse or backpack on the bus with your cell phone in it, or one of your friends is mad at you for something that's not your fault).

If you normally think or say, "I always forget my stuff," or "I can't do anything right," change your language. From now on, think and say either:

1. A personal affirmation: *"I made a mistake, but I will try to do better tomorrow,"* or
2. A spiritual affirmation: *"I can do all things through Christ who strengthens me." (Philippians 4:13 NKJV)*

When you tell yourself you're not good enough, pretty enough, or smart enough to do something, you're selling yourself short and yielding to Satan. Instead, empower yourself by saying something positive. If you practice saying and thinking the right things often enough, it will become second nature. If you're a Christian, use Scriptures as affirmations, like in the example above. Memorize specific promises from scripture and confess them out loud, changing the pronouns to make them personal. You can say and pray these affirmations during your daily quiet time (where you reflect and meditate), or anytime throughout the day. You can't over-do the positivity. Anyone can use the power of affirmations to turn negative self-thoughts into empowering thoughts.

MORE THAN MEETS THE EYE

I used to watch VH-1 and MTV all the time—back when they played music videos all day (reality TV was not yet invented). I always loved to dance, and I was a bit fanatical about watching music videos. Whether it was Janet Jackson, Paula Abdul, or Salt-N-Pepa, I was captivated. I would learn all the dance moves in the music videos that played on VH-1 and MTV by recording them (with a VCR—that was the recording device that preceded DVD players and DVRs), and replaying them over and over again. I'd simultaneously press the pause and play buttons to catch the more difficult pieces of choreography. You couldn't talk to me when one of these music videos came on TV, and it was best that the furniture was moved out of the way, because the videos instantly took me into a zone. Friends and family that came around while I was dancing found it amusing, but they knew not to mess with me.

My favorite dance video of all time is Janet Jackson's "The Pleasure Principle." I didn't have a clue what she was talking about in the song, but the video had me mesmerized. It was just her dancing in an empty warehouse, full of passion, but not wearing anything revealing or suggestive—just a cinched tee shirt, jeans, and sneakers, with her hair bone-straight. You couldn't tell me anything when that video came on, and if I did have a friend over, talking to me or playing with me, it all stopped as soon as that song came on. The coffee table got pushed to the side, and before long my glasses would fly off across the room doing those moves. The only thing I couldn't do was the back flip off the chair toward the end of the routine. To this day, I have no problem rockin' out when I see the video.

Although "The Pleasure Principle" video wasn't sexually suggestive, it was a rare breed. In those early MTV rock videos, I would constantly see images of White women with lots of cleavage and skimpy skirts, or lying around on cars. Although the color of the women in the videos may have changed, we see the same over-sexualized and blatantly violent images in hip-hop, today. It's the same routine.

In my earlier MTV-watching days, videos and songs were either played or banned. There were no "radio-friendly," edited versions without cuss words, or sexual or violent references bleeped out. Things are less black-and-white today; I'm sure you've noticed in the songs you listen to now that only some of these questionable words are edited out.

I wish I could say that the media doesn't affect us much, but it does. Over time, seeing these images and singing these words to a good beat desensitizes the best of us. We do the latest dances from the videos, pick up slang from the songs, and absorb messages about how young women should look, dress, act, or be treated by the opposite sex. Usually only light-skinned (or brown-skinned) women, hair textures (usually straight or wavy—often from a weave), sizes and shapes appear in these videos as being glamorous and desirable.

I have countless videotapes of music and awards shows that I've collected over the years. I haven't gotten around to converting them to a digital format yet, but it doesn't matter because I can still see the images in my head. If I hear any, and I mean any song that I saw a video of more than once, it plays back in my mind (especially any dance scenes). Music videos made an indelible mark on my brain. And like most kids, when I was in junior high and high school, I often tried to copy the celebrities' styles, emulating elements of those that I admired in small ways, such as my hair, clothing, and jewelry.

We know that, like models, video girls do not represent mainstream women but are just an ideal or fantasy. "Video vixens" are airbrushed and manipulated visually to keep that standard of beauty. Not that it mattered—I wanted to be one of those video girls! Of course, I didn't know then what I know now about the music business, and the Melyssa Fords and the Karrine Steffanses of the industry—video vixens that sometimes crossed the line and did some un-ladylike things to get ahead.

> **Like models, video girls do not
> represent the mainstream of women,
> but just an ideal or male fantasy.**

Did you know that some actors, singers, and rappers block the content they produce from their own kids? Even they know that subjecting someone impressionable to acts of violence, and sexually suggestive, demeaning music is detrimental to a young person's psyche. You have to guard your eyes and ears from these messages so you don't fall into temptation or become discontent with your life.

Before you turn on a movie or listen to an album, put it to the test: If you would be ashamed or embarrassed for your pastor or your grandparent to be in the room with you when you're watching or listening, you may want to think twice about doing so.

DOWN BUT NOT OUT

Sometimes you may wonder why you feel the way you do. Feelings aren't inherently wrong, but they can signify to you that something in your life needs your attention. For example, loneliness may signify that something important is missing your life, and you have to identify what that is. But how do you go about finding what you're missing? Who do you turn to for help? To find answers, you can talk about it, forgive and forget about it, or pray about it.

TALK ABOUT IT

Therapy is not taboo. Praying should not be your last resort—or your only one. Talk to an adult you trust, join a support group in your community, or see a therapist. (Therapy is not just for White folks, so dismiss that stigma and seek professional help if you need it!)

Sometimes you also have to talk yourself up, and encourage yourself because there won't always be someone around to make you feel better. Step outside yourself and think about it. If you had a friend who was going through the same thing, what would you tell her to do? Now say that same thing to yourself!

FORGIVE AND FORGET

You can't always take anger and rage at face value. Sometimes when you have these feelings, they are masking a deeper hurt. If your father is missing, someone is abusing you, or your mother is dating a man who's a jerk, you may feel that anger even if you choose to suppress it instead of displaying it. It's not wrong to feel angry; it's what you do when you're angry that makes the difference.

When it comes to betrayal or rejection, feel the anger, hurt and pain, but know that in order to get over it, you have to forgive the offender. That person may or may not apologize, or the offender may not even know he's offended you. But in either case, forgiving others helps set you free. It doesn't mean that what the person did to you was right, or that you should continue to interact with that person and trust him the way you used to. It just means letting go and moving on.

You also need to forgive yourself when you make mistakes. So often others forgive us, but we remain so hard on ourselves about a situation that we don't fully let go of the guilt. Be patient with yourself—inner growth takes time. Learn lessons along the way, and stay the course. God changes us from glory to glory—a little bit at a time.

PRAY ABOUT IT

First and foremost, understand that prayer should not be your last—or only—resort. If you do pray about your feelings but can't find the answer in God's Word, pray and ask God to speak to your heart. What do you do in the meantime? You wait. How long? Pray until something happens (PUSH). If He doesn't answer you right away and guide you on your next step, wait. Do not create your own answers. There is safety in the counsel of godly advisors, but don't confuse yourself by seeking out too many others for advice.

Nobody likes to wait, but waiting will help you develop patience and deepen your trust in God. We can't see what He's doing behind the scenes, but we can experience true freedom if we trust God completely and let it go. Let the situation rest in His hands—that means you rest your mind and let Him do the work. He doesn't need your help, and acting in haste before the right time could make the situation a lot worse.

LOVING YOU FOR *YOU*

I'm sure you've heard this before, but it bears repeating: You've got to love yourself before you can expect anyone else to. But what you don't often hear is how to love yourself.

What does a person who loves herself look like? Here are ten identifying traits:

1. *She is secure with herself.* She accepts herself as she is—flaws and all—but she seeks to gradually make improvements where practical. Wide nose, skinny legs, kinky hair—whatever others may tease her for, she is proud of and embraces herself for who she is. She knows she is a work-in-progress. She has self-confidence and doesn't feel "less than" when in the company of others who may be (or seem) more accomplished, attractive, or richer than she is.

2. *She understands her worth and acts as such.* She has a healthy self-respect, earns the respect of others with her behavior and demeanor, and expects the same in return. She doesn't allow people to waste her time, whether it's a friend, a date, or a partner in business. She doesn't settle for a romantic partner who mistreats or neglects her. She treats herself well, and pampers herself.

3. *She's healthy.* She takes care of her hygiene and enjoys things that make her look and feel good. She gets a proper amount of rest, eats a healthy diet overall, and maintains an active lifestyle. She doesn't engage in thoughtless acts of casual, unprotected sex, or reckless alcohol or drug use.

4. *She forgives herself for her mistakes.* She doesn't engage in negative self-talk or put herself down. She diffuses negative thoughts with righteous ones (affirmations). She's patient with her progress in life, setting goals and giving herself room to grow.

5. *She celebrates her successes.* She doesn't downplay her achievements and milestones. She also takes the time to enjoy the fruits of her hard work.

6. *She surrounds herself with positive, uplifting people, and limits toxic influences.* She knows her success is directly proportional to the kind of company she keeps, so she avoids or eliminates toxic people from her life who seek to take from her and give nothing in return. (Too many withdrawals without deposits will leave you with a negative balance!)

7. *She is connected to her Creator.* She spends quiet time with her Creator regularly and is aware of the soft, still voice inside her that guides her decisions.

8. *She finds time to relax and enjoy herself.* She doesn't go too long without engaging in a social activity or trip (either alone or with good friends) where she can let her hair down and have some fun.

9. *She invests in her future.* She doesn't spend more than she has (living above her means), or abuse credit. She has (or is building) an emergency fund, retirement nest egg, and follows a personal financial plan so she won't have to work all her life.

10. *She gives back to others.* She volunteers to share her time and talents, and supports charities. (Money is only one part of giving back.)

Now that you see self-love defined, where do you see yourself? How do you fare? Do you love yourself? Take some time to reflect on how you feel.

CONSIDER THIS

Courage is not the absence of fear. Courage is your resolution to do it anyway—whatever "it" is—in spite of your feelings of fear, insecurity, and doubt. You only have one heart and one mind, so take care of them.

When left unchecked, isolation, depression, secrecy and loneliness can become a breeding ground for sin to develop and take hold. The enemy works well when we're in isolation, so don't fall into his convenient trap. Instead, confide in people you trust and be honest. And if you or someone you know is having thoughts of hurting themselves, contact Suicide Awareness Voices of Education (SAVE) on their national toll-free hotline at (800) 273-TALK.

FURTHER READING
Learning who you are and finding yourself will take time.
While you reflect, check out other girls' feelings about life in Shaun Robinson's book *Exactly As I Am: Celebrated Women Share Candid Advice with Today's Girls on What it Takes to Believe in Yourself.*

4

WHAT'S **WRONG** with my eating habits?

"Nothing would be more tiresome than eating and drinking if God had not made them a pleasure as well as a necessity."

— VOLTAIRE —

My love of eating used to be (seemingly) without consequence. I was underweight for much of my life until my mid-20s. But everyone's genes (and eating habits) don't work that way. Later, I gained a lot of weight and felt terrible about myself.

Have you ever been overweight? Do you love everything about the skin you're in? Most of us don't—at least not at first. But you can overcome all of this with a positive attitude, better food choices, and an overall healthy lifestyle.

I can eat. In fact, I would say I love to eat. OK, love is a strong word, and it implies that I eat all the time. But I can eat, and I enjoy my food when I'm eating it (you can tell because I'm not a quiet eater—I'm guilty of smacking). So let's get into the ins and outs of ideal weight, your body image, exercise, and my fave—eating!

MOVE YOUR BODY

In today's fast-paced society, many of us don't cook much (if at all), and we like to eat "on the go." In fact, almost everyone I know eats in the car at some time or another, if not daily.

Once I finished high school and college, I took a job where I sat at a desk. This was contrary to the jobs I had in school, where I was used to walking everywhere, catching the city bus, and being on my feet all the time. When I moved out on my own for good, I drove everywhere and sat all day. Consequently, I moved less, gained weight, and my pants and jeans got tighter on me. I wasn't moving like I used to, but I continued eating lots of fast food on the run, and my metabolism slowed because of it. The main reason I didn't exercise was because I didn't want to sweat out my perm! I guess I didn't mind being fat as long as I had pretty hair. That was the way I used to think, because I was in denial.

The word "exercise" is not often met with enthusiasm because it sounds like work—and it is. The key is to make your body work hard while you're having fun. If you can "trick" yourself into exercising by getting into sports or activities you enjoy, then it's not so bad! I'm not into sports, but I like bowling (you don't break a sweat), dancing (you do), and kickboxing and Zumba classes (you really do). What activities do you enjoy?

WEIGHING IN

I don't recommend traditional height/weight charts that fitness experts use to assess what's healthy for you. Height/weight charts are unrealistic—they seem to be based on something other than reality. To this day, I can enter my height and weight into an online chart to calculate my body mass index (BMI), and it will tell me that I'm overweight and should weigh no more than 150 pounds. Not true! I've weighed more than 150 pounds since I was 18 and only when I hit 200 pounds did I stop feeling my best. BMI does not take into consideration your muscle mass—and muscle weighs more than fat.

I remember getting weighed at a military recruiter's office, and he said I needed to lose 30 pounds before I could come back and join the service. I was 5 feet 6 inches tall and a size 8 or 10 at most, so what was I supposed to do? Be a crackhead? I didn't lose the weight, I didn't return, and I didn't feel bad about it, either. I've gained weight in the 15 years since then, but I'm not overweight. I still look good because I take care of myself.

The beauty and entertainment industries may want you to believe that you have to be young and thin to be considered pretty, popular, or get noticed. In the Black community, however, it's more acceptable to be "thick" and have any complexion. No matter what shade you are, you can still be considered Black and be accepted as such. Our community is definitely more accepting of a variety of looks. However, I grew up in a White community, where thin was in.

I was pretty skinny in elementary school, but when I got to be about 12 or 13, my hips popped out and my butt got bigger. I was never anorexic or bulimic, but there was some pressure among my friends to be as skinny as possible. I'm not aware of any of my friends taking it to the extreme of not eating or throwing up everything they ate, but one thing is for sure, then and now: I can eat, and I'm not down with throwing up my food. I like food, so there's no point for me, but then again anorexia and bulimia are diseases that are not based on reality.

I went through a dark period where I gained 50 pounds. I was unhappy and depressed, and I just didn't care about myself the way I should have. If you find yourself in a period of depression, food is probably not the root problem for the numbers on your scale. You've got to go a little deeper under the surface to understand why you feel the way you do and why you turn to food to help you feel better (which is only temporary, unlike the extra pounds you're left with). Using food as a pacifier for your problems only makes things worse. As we discussed in the last chapter, this is where counseling or talking to an adult you trust can make a big difference.

TURNING IT AROUND

As fate would have it, I received a postcard one day in late 2004, announcing the grand opening for a weight-loss clinic nearby. The postcard was addressed to my mother (who wasn't overweight), but a few days later, on January 2, I walked into that clinic and signed up. I was about 5 feet 6 inches tall, 210 pounds, and wore a size 18.

At the time, I didn't understand how I would lose weight by eating, but that's what I was told. I received a booklet with a list of the right kinds of foods and portion sizes for my current weight and (nonexistent) activity level, a log to keep notes on everything I ate, and I bought some "cleansing" juice and protein snacks for my in-between-meals cravings. I was a little skeptical that I could reach my goal weight of 160 without exercising, but I took that first step.

A few days later the weight started coming off. I shunned tempting foods, like the cakes and goodies my sister brought home regularly, and fast food (even though it was hard to give up those McDonalds breakfast sandwiches every morning). I had a few slip-ups, but I stuck with it, and after six months, I reached my goal of losing 50 pounds! I dropped four dress sizes, and my friends could tell, starting with my face, neck, belly, and breasts (which I could have stood to keep, but oh well). Had I been moving my body with a little activity, I probably could have reached my goal faster and ate larger servings in my meals (with more activity your body requires more calories), but nevertheless, I was elated. I felt as fly as I looked!

LEARN YOUR TRIGGERS

I noticed one of the main triggers of my weight gain is carbs, such as those found in desserts, ice cream, chips, and other snacks. Carbs blow me up! I'm not crazy about sweets, but crunchy snacks—now you're talking. Salt blows me up, too, and it's most offensive to my body in frozen meals. Marie Callendar's, Lean Cuisine, Stouffers—they all are laden with sodium. I learned so much from the weight loss program I was on because I kept a food diary and weighed myself a few days a week. I learned that it was best for me to eat certain types of foods throughout the day while avoiding others in the evening, when there isn't as much time to burn it off.

I've been known to eat pasta with my meals and omit vegetables, but green vegetables are the best at keeping you healthy and also keeping you regular. (For a healthy digestive system, you should have a bowel movement at least every other day.) Processed foods, such as canned vegetables, meals prepared from a box, fast food, and meals at restaurants are also known culprits of weight gain for me. These foods are loaded with fat and salt, so if you have problems with maintaining your desired weight, start there—enjoy these foods sparingly or in moderation and end the struggle to zip up your favorite jeans.

**Processed foods and fast food
are known culprits of weight gain.**

DO IT FOR YOU

When I lost those 50 pounds, I can't begin to tell you how good I felt being able to fit into my old, "thinner" clothes and give away my "fat" clothes. I was so proud of myself, and I felt better about myself. Losing weight is something I did for me—not to please someone else, make someone like me or treat me differently, or attract someone as a mate. I did it because I, Daree, wanted to!

It's never a good idea to lose weight or change your appearance in any way just to please someone else. You need to listen to yourself and not let others' comments influence you to go against what will make you happy and feel better about yourself.

CONSIDER THIS

The keys to good health are moderation and prevention. Doing anything in excess is not healthy—whether it's eating too much junk food or candy, or exercising for three hours a day and eating nothing but green salads (and I'm talking ordinary people here, not athletes in training, or people who have a strict, doctor-approved dietary regimen for a good reason).

**The keys to good health are
moderation and prevention.**

Daree's Diet Do's

At restaurants: Ask for a to-go box when you order your entree (unless you're just having an appetizer). When the food arrives, immediately put half your meal in the box, take it home, and don't eat it until the next day.

At home: Make your own "100-calorie" snack by pouring chips, popcorn, or whatever it is into a small bowl, instead of (mindlessly) eating it straight out of the bag. If you get the 100-calorie bags from the store, good luck with not eating more than one, which will defeat the purpose. (I don't mess with them—they're just small enough to make me mad because so many can be eaten in just a few bites.)

Whenever you have the choice, select healthy options:

- Look for fruit and other healthy snacks to downplay some of the junk food.
- Prepare your meals by baking, boiling, or broiling instead of frying. Add flavor with herbs, spices, marinades, and seasonings other than salt.
- Try low-fat, low-sodium versions of processed foods you already like. Edy's, for example, has a "Slow Churned" version of their ice cream with less fat—but when you're eating it, trust me, all the flavor is still there. I wouldn't lie to you. Land O' Lakes has a low-sodium version of their white American cheese, and you can't tell the difference. And what about some chicken soup for the soul? There are reduced-sodium versions of soup everywhere —I promise you won't miss the salt they took out. (Fat-free foods are more of a risk in my opinion because the flavor usually suffers. Plus, fat-free usually equals high-carb.)

For those who complain that healthy foods are more expensive, I can agree that some food options may cost more in the short run. But I'd rather pay a little more for my organic milk now than have health issues and take several expensive prescriptions to undo the damage of eating and living an unhealthy (cheaper, more convenient) lifestyle. You decide. I don't think you have to cut all "bad" foods, but start modifying your diet with small changes until you find a balance that works for you. Everything in moderation, folks.

My suggestion for those of you struggling with your weight is to keep a food diary of everything you eat, including how it was cooked, what time you ate it, how you were feeling, and any activity that you did during the day that could be considered exercise. Weigh yourself two to three times a week at the same time each day. In this way, you can learn your body's patterns of weight gain and loss, and your food triggers. Also take note of the days of your menstrual cycle, as your period will impact your weight fluctuation. Check out "Daree's Diet Do's" (in the sidebar) for more tips and tricks on how to prepare and make healthier food choices.

Learn to accept your body type, move it regularly, and eat right (fast food/candy in moderation). These are the best ways to achieve and maintain your ideal weight. I've never looked as heavy as I am, but I knew when I didn't feel right. Get to know your body and your ideal weight range for yourself.

Accepting your body type, moving it regularly, and eating right are the best ways to achieve and maintain your ideal weight.

Diseases like anorexia and bulimia start with a distorted mentality. I urge you, if you are having problems with the way you look at food or have lost the joy in eating to the point where you have no desire to eat, get professional help. The National Eating Disorders Association has a toll-free confidential helpline at (800) 931-2237. For books and other resources about eating disorders, go to www.bulimia.com.

FURTHER READING

When you're shopping for groceries, feast your eyes on David Zinczenko and Matt Goulding's book, *Eat This, Not That! 2011: Thousands of Easy Food Swaps that Can Save You 10, 20, 30 Pounds—or More!* It gives great guidelines on how to read labels on processed foods.

part two

YOUR RELATIONSHIPS—CAN YOU RELATE?

5

WHAT'S **WRONG** with my family?

"Feelings of worth can flourish only in an atmosphere where individual differences are appreciated, mistakes are tolerated, communication is open, and rules are flexible—the kind of atmosphere that is found in a nurturing family."

— **VIRGINIA SATIR** —

You can choose your friends, but you can't choose your family. You have no control over how you're raised. The influence of parents is undeniably strong, just as how much our family environment shapes us.

It's interesting how the lives of children raised in the same household can turn out so differently when they become adults. It goes to show you that nature versus nurture is no argument—how we develop is a product of both. Whether you live in a household with nuclear, blended, or extended family members, you can't deny that families are as complex and diverse as we are.

This chapter discusses my family life as a girl, and my biggest influence in that regard was undeniably my dad. His nickname for me was "Ree Ree," and then it changed to "Ree" as I grew up. I regard them both as terms of endearment. I tried hard to win his approval and see some outward expression of love toward me. I hope you can learn something from my story.

REE REE IN THE MIDDLE

Have you ever noticed that the behavioral dynamics between you and your parents are different from that of your siblings? Sometimes we may think of children being treated differently by their parents as favoritism, but birth order has a lot to do with it as well.

As the middle child of three, I would often get caught in the middle (pun intended). In literally the same moment, my mother could scold me for something having to do with my little sister, but my older brother could tease me mercilessly and get away with it. To this day, when it comes to family, I often alternate between staying to myself and playing "peacemaker."

My sister looked up to me when we were young, and everyone always thought she was so cute. People would always compliment my mother about how beautiful she was.

I always looked up to my brother. I was told that as a baby, he was the only one who could make me laugh.

DYSFUNCTION, SECRETS, AND LONGING

I could often sense the conflict between my brother and my dad. Unfortunately, I noticed their dysfunction with each other easily, long before I had ever heard of the word 'dysfunction' or knew how to spell it. When my brother was about 16, he moved to my gramma's house for awhile because of some issues with my dad, and I missed him terribly (she lived in Albany, NY, about 90 miles away). I always looked forward to his visits. At one point I think he got really depressed and took a bunch of pills. Shortly after that, my mom told me he was in the hospital but wouldn't explain much.

September 3, 1990, 10:04 p.m.
My brother is in the hospital. I don't know why.
Mom said he and Dad had a long talk and now
their differences are settled. And he's gonna come
back and live here from now on. He was just
confused about some things.

At least that was what I was told at the time.

I didn't fully understand it then, but around 14 or 15, I learned that my brother was actually my 'half-brother.' (I don't like that term, but it's technically correct.) My parents got married when my brother was three, after which time my dad adopted him and changed his full legal name. My brother remained in touch with his biological father, whom also got married and had several other children (with who he remained in touch). My brother struggled for my father's acceptance, as did I, although for different reasons. However, I remember him getting special things from his biological father's family for years, while my sister and I were left out, and I didn't know why—my mother didn't openly talk about it or explain that they were my brother's "other family."

When we were young, my dad seemed to have a more playful and relaxed relationship with my sister than with me. They would do fun things together without me, and I didn't like him because of it. I felt like he only paid attention to me when he was yelling at me or telling me what to do.

I felt helpless about my feelings. I wanted my dad to say that he loved me and I wanted him to show me his love by taking me places or talking to me like he did with her, but I was too fearful to tell him. I didn't know the right way to say it back then, and he wasn't the most approachable person (think of the antithesis of Bill Cosby's role as Cliff Huxtable on *The Cosby Show*). I carried those needs with me as I got older and involved myself with guys who were emotionally unavailable because that's how my dad was to me.

Do you ever feel like your emotional needs are ignored by the people you love? What happens when you reach out to them? Our interactions with loved ones are profoundly strong in shaping our self-esteem.

MY ROCK

Do you ever butt heads with your mom? Or are you two the best of friends? Maybe you even look like sisters. The mother-daughter relationship is also a complex one, no doubt. Mom is usually the one who, by her actions, teaches us how to become successful, intelligent women (or conversely, what not to do). But I cannot imagine my life without my mother always being there. She was a rock, even when she didn't know it and considered herself weak.

> **I cannot imagine my life without my mother in it. She was a rock.**

My mother is a low-key woman, and as a child I remember the feeling of safety and security I always felt when she was around. If we were apart for any long period of time, such as when she went to work or I went to school, she always made me feel like she was so happy to see me once she returned to me, and I felt the same way.

I remember myself being an obedient child, but she tells me I was very strong-willed (I know I am now!). I often felt misunderstood by her, but she was always patient with me. She has a gift to encourage others, listen to their problems, and give them advice if they want it (without butting in), but she didn't always stand up for herself.

My mother often took us kids to our gramma's house in Albany, which was a 90-minute car ride away. I remember times when my dad wouldn't let my mom take the car to visit her, so we all had to catch the Greyhound bus. There were also years when she had no car at all, and she caught the city bus to and from work at all hours, while my dad always had a new, leased car.

As I became a teen, I started to become more observant. I noticed that my mother's personality came alive with her friends and family, but that she was low-key, somewhat introverted and submissive around my father. She was prone to depression and she often put on a front, trying to pretend that things were OK even when they were not.

July 24, 1990, 10:36 p.m.

An hour ago, my parents were fighting in the kitchen while we were in the living room. It had something to do with the house and the dishes. Dad was yelling but Mom kept calm.

Dad: This house looks like a Goddamn pig pen!
Mom: What do you mean by that?
—Silence—
Mom: I wanna know what you mean by that.
—Silence—
Mom: Don't talk to me like I'm a child—swearin' and carryin' on...

I didn't get it, because our house was never messy—sometimes my room was, but overall it wasn't bad. Me and my sister went upstairs because she was getting upset, so I didn't hear the rest. But I'm proud of Mom for setting Dad straight and not backing down.

April 29, 1991, 5:16 p.m.
My parents are getting divorced...
I couldn't be happier.

At age 14, I heard a rumor that my parents were getting divorced, which I was happy about because of all the tension surrounding interactions with my dad. But it wasn't true. They didn't divorce until I was 30 years old with a child of my own (and also divorcing—which I'll discuss later.) She said she stayed with him all those years even when she was unhappy because she wanted us kids to be taken care of, and she didn't think she could do it on her own. It's thoughts like that that keep me determined to make it right now as a single mother.

At the time, I felt like her marriage and us kids were a mistake, and that she must feel trapped living with such a controlling man. But there are many aspects of their marriage that I didn't know about, and I probably would not have understood even if knew the details back then. What I do know is that my siblings and I hated seeing her unhappy.

Have you ever stopped to think about the sacrifices your parents make for your good? Don't take them for granted.

THE MAN OF THE HOUSE

My personality was more like my dad's than my mom's, and when people tell me that, they don't mean it as a compliment. It's often said that a girl's greatest influence when growing up is her father, or a father figure. I was no different. The root of my daddy issues is easy to spot.

Dad was strict. Can you say authoritarian? He didn't have a lot of words for us unless he was in a playful mood, which was unpredictable. When us kids would go to him to ask for permission to do something, he would often answer with a grunt, or maybe one word if we were lucky. On the occasions that we could do or get what we asked for, he'd say two words: "Go 'head." But many times, we would just stand in front of him, looking and feeling stupid while he took his time thinking about it. If he didn't answer us then, we'd have to go away and come back. He definitely had a compartmentalized, analytical mind.

My dad never went to church with the rest of us. I've only seen him in church for a few weddings and funerals—that's it. He had my brother teach me to say grace and bedtime prayers from a book, and he had his own Bible, but I didn't even know if he was a Christian for a long time (he is, but I couldn't tell).

My dad is from Pittsburgh, Pennsylvania, and comes from a large family with six brothers and sisters. On one rare occasion, his siblings, nieces and nephews came from Pittsburgh to our house in New York when I was about eight, and I was at the kitchen table at dinnertime, eating and talking with the rest of my cousins. He called me into the living room where he was eating in front of the TV. I walked up to him, not knowing why he called me, and without saying a word, he punched me dead in my stomach. It hurt so bad that I immediately started crying quiet tears—I could hardly breathe for my sobs. I walked back to my seat in the kitchen, and no one said anything to him or me. I guess that was my punishment for talking too much.

When Dad would go out of town on trips, my siblings and I would celebrate and let our hair down. The tension in the house evaporated without my father around. Mom didn't travel much without us, but when she did, I missed her terribly, and I wanted Dad to miss her too. He didn't seem to care, but how would we know if he did? He almost never showed any loving emotion.

IN CONTROL

My dad exerted control without contest in my early years. There was no question who was in charge in our household. Often, I didn't understand what the big deal was and why he didn't let me do things that seemed harmless.

After numerous requests, my dad finally allowed me to get my ears pierced for the first time on the day after I graduated from the sixth grade (I was 11). When I was 14, I wanted to take dance classes, and he said, "No, you must be crazy." I ended up getting my mom's to agree to take me to and from the classes and pay my weekly tuition on the condition that I pay her back when I got a job. When I started working at age 15, I kept that promise. But even with money of my own, my dad wouldn't allow me to get contact lenses, so I had to wait until I went away to college at 17. I never understood the reasoning behind any of these decisions, but I was not allowed to question him. At that time, I chalked it up to him being a control freak. That's probably one of the reasons why I'm such an independent woman now.

OUT OF CONTROL

I attended the University of Albany (SUNY Albany) for my sophomore year and lived with my gramma for the first semester. It was NOT my idea. She is a very opinionated, negative person and unpleasant to be around. I wanted to stay at the University of Buffalo (SUNY Buffalo, otherwise known as "UB,") where I spent my freshman year, but when my dad learned that the dorms were co-ed, he nixed that arrangement.

One night when I was 19, I was out late with my boyfriend Kevin at his sister's house, and when I came back to my gramma's house, I couldn't get in. I had a key to the bottom lock on the doorknob, but not the deadbolt. She actually locked me out of the house two nights that week. After the second time, my aunt gave me a spare key she had for the deadbolt. With that crazy situation and others, I told my parents I wanted to move out and get an apartment with Kevin. They didn't approve because we weren't married, but I was clear that I was leaving Gramma's house regardless. Within a couple of months, I got my first apartment alone, and I broke up with Kevin shortly thereafter (I'll talk more about my relationship with Kevin as we go along).

WHATCHA GOT COOKIN'?

I caught the bus to school when I was in high school—I think I had to be in homeroom by 7:10 a.m., but I have never been a morning person. Thankfully, Mom always hooked us up. After waking us up in a gentle tone, she would sometimes make breakfast. My favorite breakfast on school days was Cream of Wheat. She would have bowls set out for my siblings and I, ready to go with the steam still rising up, sugar already swirled in, and a square of butter lying on top, melting in the middle and then rolling into the sides of the bowl for as long as it took for us to come downstairs and get it. Cream of Wheat for me was the kind of breakfast that "sticks to your ribs" and it kept me from feeling starved—at least for a little while.

I think breakfast foods were the first that I learned to cook. A lot of things that I cooked while I was growing up were not from scratch, however. I made a lot of boxed dinners like Kraft macaroni and cheese. I didn't learn how to make real macaroni and cheese—the kind that you bake—until I was an adult. I only made that stuff because it's what I saw my mother do. Gramma taught her how to cook, but Mom rarely cooked the kind of foods Gramma did, and not from scratch.

Gramma is from Montgomery, Alabama and she's old-school. She knows how to cook everything and her Thanksgiving dinners were especially memorable. Every year, she would cook for days prior, shooing my uncles out of the kitchen when they tried to sneak a taste. When the food was ready, we would set the dining room table with the "good" china, and sit watching us eat. She said it gave her satisfaction to watch us tear up her food. Since Thanksgiving prep kept her in the kitchen all day, she was never hungry at dinnertime.

Gramma's cooking wasn't a big deal to her since she always cooks for herself. She didn't love her cooking the way we did. She said sometimes you get used to your own food and other people's cooking tastes better. She would rave about how delicious my cooking was, even though I made stuff from a box! I used to think, 'Gramma thinks my food is the bomb? The best cook is telling me that my food is all that? Really?' But she meant it. And since Gramma is not generous with compliments, it meant a lot to me.

Someone else who wasn't so generous with approval was my dad. He is not exactly known for praising anyone. There are so few times that I felt or heard my father's approval, and those rare times when I did, it meant the world to me, whether I was 5, 15, or 25. I desperately needed to know that he loved me and approved of me.

When I was about 10 or so, I was excited to make dinner (I don't remember what it was). I anxiously waited to get my dad's reaction, but he didn't readily give his opinion or make any comments. So I asked, "Dad, is it any good? Do you like it?"

He barely looked up and replied gruffly, "I'm eating it, ain't I?" And that was one of my first compliments from my critical, analytical dad.

Many years later, my then-husband and I prepared Thanksgiving dinner for the first time—the turkey, all the trimmings and fixin's—at our new home in Upper Marlboro, Maryland. My family came down from Baltimore, Maryland and Utica, New York, and we had a great time. (I think it was my birthday too—every six years, my birthday is on Thanksgiving Day.) Once everyone had their second and third helpings, Dad got up and looked at the remaining leftovers (there wasn't much), and in front of everyone he said, "Good job, kids."

A LITTLE APPROVAL MEANS A LOT

A few years ago, the family got together for a cookout at my brother's and sister-in-law's house in Maryland, located about halfway between where my dad lived, and where the rest of us (myself, my daughter, my sister and my mom) lived in Virginia. The next day, my dad woke up early and left before any of us woke up, but not before sending an email to my siblings and I that said,

"*I love you and I'm proud of you.*
Dad"

You can't imagine how I felt when I read that, and I was an adult. I don't know if my dad will ever verbally say those three little words to me before death parts us, and I know he loves me because of his actions, not his lack of words. He calls when it's my birthday, he sends cards, and occasionally he visits, even though he typically stays less than two whole days. A little approval goes a long way. It means a lot.

People can express their feelings with actions, not just words. I often want to hear words of affirmation or affection, but I accept his way, too. Actions speak louder than words, so if my dad chooses to use acts of service to convey his love for me, I'd rather take it than leave it.

If someone tells me one thing but does something different, that makes them a hypocrite. But if they say nothing, and do something (surprising me like my dad), how bad is that? The consistent actions of a person show you who they are.

I don't always agree with the way my dad treated us as family, and I don't understand everything, but I have forgiven him for what he failed to give me emotionally. Not to make excuses, but you can't give something that you don't have. Now that I'm older, I reach out to my dad, and he may not always meet me halfway, but he will take a few steps toward me, and he accepts me.

SHOWING YOUR LOVE

One of the things I've come to understand and accept is that there are some people whose love, attention, or approval you want or need, but they may give it to you in ways you don't expect, or don't want to accept. Maybe they had a small love tank, or no role models to show them how to give, receive, or show affection. Maybe it's just their personality. Maybe their love language is different from yours. We all show love differently.

People may express their love, attention, or approval in ways you don't expect.

Speaking of love languages, there are five as described by Dr. Gary Chapman in his book *The Five Love Languages* (words of affirmation, quality time, acts of service, physical touch, and gifts). It's important that while you identify your own pretty easily, when you're dealing with others, you have to relate to them in their love language if you want them to feel loved by you. The way you show love is not always the best way for someone to receive it, so if you don't know someone's love language, ask.

If you don't know someone's love language, ask.

CONSIDER THIS

Sometimes we can "get into it" with family members like no one else. You can count on the people that you are the closest to you to make you pretty mad at times. But when it comes to our parents, we need to obey and respect them—even if they don't seem to respect us. Even if what they tell us to do (or what we can't do) doesn't seem to make any sense.

Obey and respect your parents, even if it seems like they don't respect you.

I admit that it's frustrating when you feel like you can't get a break, or you're being treated unfairly. If you think they are wrong about something they say or the way they treat you, don't fight against them so hard or cop an attitude. Instead, calm down and offer a compromise or request a "try-out," and respectfully make your appeal. If it doesn't work, you may not like it, but you still have to accept it.

At times your parents' attitudes, opinions, and behaviors may be wrong, even if you use the right approach, and you will have to pray. Pray that your heart does not become bitter and that you do not disobey them or misbehave in response to your interaction with them. It's OK to feel however you feel about something, but what you do in response is the key. You never know what is motivating your parent to act the way they do, or say what they've said—their beliefs, upbringing, current struggles, or fears can affect their judgment. So while you're on your knees, pray for them, too. They need God's help to deal with you and your siblings too—please believe it! Check your own attitude and make sure you're not setting off any red flags. You can choose to respond in a positive way no matter what they say.

It's not about how you feel, but what you do in response.

Your parents may or may not be considered 'cool' by your standards, but they don't have to be your friends. They don't need for you to like them or agree with them. They are in charge whether you want to accept it or not. But let's talk about your need for acceptance from your peers—it's normal, but it need not cause you so much dread or anxiety, nor should it take over your sense of self and individuality.

FURTHER READING

For another take on family life with lots of ups and downs to boot, have a look-see at rapper and actress Queen Latifah's book *Put On Your Crown: Life-Changing Moments on the Path to Queendom*, which is a lot like this chapter: you get great stories about her own perspective about her life's successes and failures, with a lot of family involvement.

WHAT'S **WRONG** with my friends?

> "A successful person is one who can
> lay a firm foundation with the bricks
> that others throw at him or her."
>
> — **DAVID BRINKLEY** —

The word "friend" is an overused catch-all phrase. Calling someone your friend could mean various things: an acquaintance, a casual sex partner, or a person who helps you and/or shares things and experiences with you. We all have struggles with friendships throughout life.

I had a hard time keeping good friends. I felt that I didn't have enough in common with the kids I wanted to be friends with. I told myself that kids were missing out if they didn't want to be my friends, but it really felt like the other way around. Sometimes I wondered if no one liked me because I didn't like me. What you project about yourself and how you feel about yourself comes out in your body language even if you don't talk about it.

"What about your friends?
Will they stand their ground,
or will they let you down again?
What about your friends?
Are they gonna be on down,
or will they ever be around...
or will they turn their backs on you?"
—TLC, "What About Your Friends?"

In addition to my experience with friendships, in this chapter I'll also discuss how to deal with "mean girls," how to choose the right kind of friends, and how to keep from being discouraged when you lose friends (or have to cut them off yourself).

A LONER

Sometimes I wonder what kind of person I would be if I had grown up in Pittsburgh with a host of aunts, uncles, and cousins—where my dad's side of the family is from. As a girl, I felt like I was missing out. Other people went to school with their siblings or cousins who were their instant friends— friends who would stand up for them if there were any issues with other kids at school—but not me. I always wondered what it would be like to have that.

Since I was the middle child, spaced out five to six years apart from both of my siblings, we never went to the same schools at the same time. It wasn't until 12th grade when I learned that one of my classmates was my cousin (a boy I'd known since the seventh grade, and liked, too)! Holidays were boring with nowhere to go because my whole family lived in the same house—our extended family was far away, so we just spent Christmas in the house all day every year.

MY BFFS

Too often it seemed like my girlfriends from school liked me one day, and we got along great, but the next day they would act jealous and talk about me—even my so-called "best friends."

My first best friend was a girl named Kim. She is six months older than me to the day. We met when we were four years old. We were neighbors, and best friends throughout elementary school. Sometimes she acted like she hated me, and other times she seemed to love me. We shared a lot of things with each other, but she often would talk about me behind my back, blab about something I told her in confidence, or make fun of me.

Another girl named Deanna was my best friend from the seventh to 10th grade. She lived a few blocks from me, and our parents knew each other (my mother worked for her father after we finished high school). Because of her religion, she was not allowed to wear pants, and could not go to the movies (although she could watch the same movies on TV). In spite of our religious differences, we were very close. Although I felt like I could talk to Deanna about anything and everything, sometimes I still felt empty and inadequate. Deanna liked me for who I was, even when I stressed her out. I argued with her quite a bit as our friendship progressed because of my fears. I always had a fear of someone liking me and then after I started to like them, they'd leave me and stop being my friend. I felt like I had to impress her or make her laugh so she'd continue to be my friend. I'd feel threatened just because she was friendly with everyone. I was afraid she would like another girl better than me, and then I would lose my best friend. I had a lot of insecurities, and at times that came out as controlling behavior. I needed to learn to accept myself and be comfortable being myself around others. I eventually learned to stop being possessive and smothering her (she was my best friend, not my girlfriend). Just having fun is the way to go. I'm still friends with Deanna to this day; I was in her wedding, and we remain in touch.

**Learn to accept yourself
as you are and be comfortable
being yourself around others.**

Around the 10th or 11th grade, I started hanging out with a White girl named Jennifer who accepted me for who I was. Although I lived in a nicer part of town that was predominantly White, and Jennifer lived in the "ghetto" part of town, she was my first White BFF. The reason Jennifer and I became close was because of a falling out with what you would call "mean girls" or "gossip girls."

GOSSIP GIRLS

These days, I like to say that a hater is a motivator. But back in the day, I didn't see it that way.

I remember hanging out with a group of friends including Kim, Deanna, and Ayana, and we were pretty tight from the seventh to the 10th grade, but things came to a head in 11th grade: One of the funniest, boldest, and most outspoken girls in the group, Ayana, considered me uppity and claimed I thought I was too good for them and was trying to "act like a White girl" because of the way I talked and what she perceived to be my "I'm-better-than-you" attitude. Kim and Ayana's sister sided with her, while Ayana's cousin and Deanna remained friends with me (but not as close as before). It was during this time that I started hanging out with Jennifer.

Mean girls, gossip girls, bullies, b*tches—they'll always be around. Girls' reasons for being mean vary—they could be insecure, not getting enough of the right kind of attention at home, and they may even be victims of abuse. Regardless of why they treat others the way they do, your reaction and response to their antics will make the difference in the drama-meter of your day.

Mean girls like to see that their words and behavior affect you. If you react to them, showing that they're hurting your feelings or bothering you, it gives them the power and satisfaction to keep it up. In many cases, their own source of self-esteem is putting others down and getting attention from it.

Mean girls like to see that their words and behavior affect you.

You don't have to answer to name-calling. If someone addresses you by anything but your name, you don't have to answer (in fact, you probably shouldn't). Often, ignoring the mean girl is the best way to go (at least hold out until you get home to cry or complain about it).

Don't talk about the mean girl to her friends or with any of them around. If you choose to stop ignoring her and confront her, take note. Confrontations are best done one-on-one because there's less pressure on both of you. Don't be defensive; just be honest. Confronting her in the company of others gives her attention, so you have to be ready if you really want to battle with her (and hopefully you keep it verbal—not physical). Please—walk away from the threat of a physical fight. The emotional scars won't heal when your skin does.

I was able to mature and grow out of my teenage angst. During the last weeks of high school, I wrote in my diary:

June 2, 1994, 8:13 p.m.
I've gotten acquainted with everyone I wanted to in the past three years. I've grown so much emotionally, and the turmoil with my ex-best friends has made me stronger.

KEEP YOUR CIRCLE TIGHT AND RIGHT

Everyone can't be on your front row. A few close friends are more than enough. Choose positive friends, even if they're not the most popular. It's likely that you'll be laughed at and ridiculed for doing what's right, so you'll need supporters to walk that positive, upright lifestyle with you to encourage you. Think about and look for people who have the same mindset as you, and befriend them.

For example, if some of the girls you hang out with smoke, it doesn't mean you should try it. If anything, you should reconsider your friendship with them. Or maybe there is a group of popular girls who are promiscuous. Just because they engage in sexual acts doesn't mean you should, but if you hang around them, the pressure to do what they are doing will intensify. Don't underestimate the power of influence. If a bunch of people in your circle of influence are doing something, it won't be long before you go there, too (this applies to good and bad behavior). Maybe you need to move them to the acquaintance category and not keep them so close—just say, "What's up?" in the hallways and keep it moving.

When it comes to the people we spend time with, we must be careful of their influence on us. In 1 Corinthians 15:33, Paul warns us about bad influences. How can you protect yourself from other people's bad morals and prevent them from corrupting you?

- ☞ Set boundaries. A boundary is an intangible emotional and intellectual line that is established in relationships for freedom, protection, and privacy. Be prepared in advance, because when you get into the situation it may be too late to make a quality decision. *(We'll discuss boundaries more when we talk about dating in the next chapter.)*
- ☞ Do not closely associate with people who enjoy gossip or arguments. These people are toxic and can "infect" you if you have prolonged exposure and you do not detach from them, and they should be avoided *(see Romans 16:17 and Proverbs 6:16, 19)*.
- ☞ Discourage certain behavior in your presence: smoking, swearing, certain types of movies/TV programming *(see Romans 12:2)*.
- ☞ Do not let other's poor treatment of you determine or influence how you treat them. Treat them how you want to be treated, with a pure heart, regardless of what they say or do.

CHECKMATE

It is prudent to take a look at the people you interact with, and periodically assess which of the four levels, or categories of friendship you have placed them in: intimate friends, close friends, casual friends, and acquaintances:

Acquaintances—Acquaintances are people that you know in some way, but you have no intention of pursuing a closer friendship with them. This will be your largest friendship category, because it consists of everyone you know, whether you actually consider them a friend or not.

Casual —This group consists of people we see regularly (for example, at work, in the neighborhood, or in classes). A real friendship hasn't developed with any of these people because you don't share much of yourself with them. Typically you'll have about 20-100 people in this category.

Close—You'll probably have about 10-30 or more people in this category, as follows:

• Associates—those you become close to because you both have a specific job or place of service.

• Mentors—those who build significantly into your life by teaching, counseling, and guiding you.

• Personal friends—the ones you see, talk to, or spend time with frequently, by mutual choice. You are comfortable sharing bits and pieces of who you really are with them.

Intimate—You feel at home with intimate friends without fear or hesitation. These are the friends you trust the most and share everything with. They know all about you and love you anyway! You can lean on them in bad times, have fun with them, and they're always there for you. This is your inner circle, and this should be your smallest friendship group (usually about 3-6 maximum).

Take some time to figure out the people who influence you the most, those closest to you, and those you hang out with regularly. You may need to reevaluate a friendship and move that person to a different category. Some friendships are only meant for a season, not to hang on to for life. It takes some reflection and spiritual guidance to determine the difference between a "seasonal" friend and a lifelong one.

Make a chart with two columns (see the sample in the sidebar): one column for the category you have placed them in currently, and the category they should be in, based on the information in this section and your own reflective analysis.

Under the Influence

MY FRIENDS NOW	CURRENT FRIENDSHIP STATUS	IDEAL FRIENDSHIP STATUS
~✺ Lisa	~✺ Close	~✺ Acquaintance
~✺ Joanne	~✺ Intimate	~✺ Casual
~✺ Melissa	~✺ Casual	~✺ Close
~✺ John	~✺ Acquaintance	~✺ Acquaintance
~✺ Deidre	~✺ Close	~✺ Intimate

There's a Scripture where God tells Samuel, "...The LORD does not look at the things human beings look at. People look at the outward appearance, but the LORD looks at the heart" (1 Samuel 16:7b, NIV). Don't just look at a person for what they seem to be on the outside, but consider their personality and how they treat others (this goes for girls you want to be friends with, and guys you're interested in, too).

IT'S LONELY AT THE TOP

It takes a lot of courage to be the first person to take a stand when no one else will speak up against something wrong. If the people you admire want to be liked, or those who are considered "popular" in your school are in the wrong, it's easy to keep quiet or just go with the flow and do what everyone else is doing. It doesn't matter how old you are— right is right and wrong is wrong. You may not feel like drawing attention to yourself, but if you're a Christian, you're called to a higher standard.

Are you afraid to step out and do something bold, new, or exciting because of what others might say? Often when you're on the right path, others can't go with you, and you may feel alone, but you're not—God is leading you to a better place in your life. Pastor Paula White preached a sermon in 2006 called "I'm Back!" that addressed this idea:

> *"When you get a Word, you have to work it out in your life, then it becomes real and the enemy [Satan] comes. You will be isolated and disconnected from others. You will miss your former associations and feel like you don't fit in anywhere. This causes a hunger for a connection to God. ...It's good that people let you go, because this is a job for Jesus. Training always happens in the wilderness. ...Don't listen to the criticism or the praise—just keep walking the path. People will be fickle! In the end, you're gonna thank God for all the people who hurt you because they drew you closer. 'Judas' [the one who betrays you] is your friend!"*

Be thankful for your enemies.
They'll help you get closer to God.

Remember when I mentioned that mean girls become jealous when good things happen to you? What Pastor White is saying is that people who you thought were your friends may hurt your feelings, talk about you, and accuse you of negative behavior, but these people actually help you because they push you into your destiny—you cannot continue to stay close to people who want to drag you down—

you cannot thrive and develop into the person God has called you to be when you remain in a toxic friendship or relationship. Some people will put you down when you accomplish things, just because of their own insecurities. As much as you may care about your friends, you can only do so much for them. Don't let your feelings of guilt or longing to belong enable them or allow their manipulation to take advantage of you.

CONSIDER THIS

Friendships change, just like seasons, with different ebbs and flows. Some relationships come and go. It's normal throughout life. It's hard to find real, true friends, but we all need them.

> *"Friends will let you down, Friends won't be around*
> *When you need them most, where are your friends?*
> *Friends are hard to find, Friends—yours and mine,*
> *I'm talkin' 'bout your friends."*
> *—Jody Watley, "Friends"*

When you do the right things in life (making the right decisions and not following the crowd), you'll be blessed, but you'll also be disliked and talked about. I remember when people would talk about me (and not always behind my back), saying things like "She thinks she's all that," when good things happened in my life, or "She's trying to be White," because of the way I talked. It may start as just one person, and then others follow suit because they're afraid, jealous or insecure. If this happens, it's important for you to uphold your values and standards. Strive to stay above it.

Be careful when you form friendships in general. Do it gradually. Don't start off telling someone all your personal business right off the bat. That person has to prove he or she is trustworthy and deserving of your friendship.

Don't be too clingy, either. Clingy people are insecure and always looking to another person for approval and personal validation. Every other phrase is a question about them: "How does my hair look?" "Does this make me look fat?" "Why didn't you wait for me after class?" "Do you like her better than me?" All the constant questioning gets tiring pretty quickly.

If you feel like you don't have real friends, why not look for someone else who needs a friend? The girl who eats lunch by herself, or the shy one who always looks down when you pass her in the hallway, or the one who mean girls make fun of because of her hairstyle or the way she dresses? She would probably welcome making a new, sincere friend like you.

A true friend loves at all times. There are seasons of friend-ship, and everyone you meet can't (and shouldn't) be a close friend. Use a discerning heart to determine the type of people you should spend your time with—those who lift you up and who you feel make you better just for knowing them. Nurture those relationships and build bonds with the people who are truly there for you and care about you (you can tell when someone cares about you—they're genuine and not selfish; they're not constantly trying to take advantage you).

Don't underestimate the value of having the right people in your life. Toxic relationships, friendships, and family members drain your energy and—if you're not careful—can make you lose sight of your focus, distorting it. With some people, there comes a time to stop trying to be their friend and let them go. Toxic people will only bring you down.

Don't underestimate the value of having the right people in your life. Your friends can make you or break you.

When you grow, everyone doesn't grow with you. Be a positive example, and never lose sight of your God-given purpose. As God told Jeremiah, "For I know the plans I have for you,... plans to give you a hope and a future." (Jeremiah 29:11 NIV) He doesn't ask us to do things that we can do on our own because He won't get the glory for it. He doesn't give us assignments that are easy. We have to go through hard times so we can learn to trust Him and rely on Him. In times like this, He shows us His faithfulness and He gets the glory. Be a light that draws others to Him—and people will naturally be drawn to you as well.

Why get caught up in the he-said/she-said stuff? Who cares who's messing with whom? You're above that nonsense. Stay focused on God and your studies. Treat people right—even friends who turn out to be phonies or haters. A hater is a motivator. I know it hurts sometimes when you're going through it, but when you're 25 or 35, you'll look back on these petty situations (if you can even remember them) and see that they don't matter.

Above all, remember you can't change how other people act. You can't make a person like you or be your friend, but don't give anyone a reason not to. The way you treat people is so important. How you talk to people, your tone of voice—all the little things do matter. Don't say anything you would be embarrassed to repeat onstage in an auditorium of people or printed in a newspaper. Watch your language, be respectful of others, and when it comes to school, do what you came to do—learn.

FURTHER READING

Pepa (neé Sandy Denton) from the female hip hop group Salt-N-Pepa can attribute much of her fame to the friends and acquaintances she hung out with as a teenager. Peep her memoir, *Let's Talk About Pep* for a fun, can't-put-it-down story of a woman who endured self-esteem issues, abuse, and near-death, but triumphed over it all with much success.

WHAT'S **WRONG** with *guys?*

"If you're in the phase of getting to know someone, hold on to your heart. Notice who the person is. Look at his behavior and character."

— **HENRY CLOUD** —

July 17, 1990, 2:50 a.m.
I wonder when a boy will kiss me.
Seems like everyone else has a boyfriend but me.

I never thought of myself as pretty, so if someone said I was—especially a guy who was popular and/or good-looking—I thought, "Wow!" I put a lot of weight on guys' opinions, letting their comments determine a large part of my self-esteem instead of getting it from my relationship with God or from loving myself just as I am. Whenever I got involved with a guy, I let his words and actions toward me determine my attitude and mood for the day. I don't know why I gave guys that much power in the first place, instead of empowering myself.

July 21, 1990, 12:43 a.m.

*I've been thinking about my future, and it doesn't
look great to me. I can only judge from my past
experiences. I am very negative. I think that no boy
will ever want to go out with me (that I actually like).*

I was a late bloomer. In high school, the boys I liked didn't like me, but they liked my friends. I went to the senior ball (prom) with a friend of mine from church because he was friends with some people at my school; not because he liked me. Believe it or not, although I talked to guys here and there, I didn't have my first boyfriend until after I graduated from high school, and he just so happened to be the first guy I ever kissed or had sex with. (I'll talk more about sex, and why it may not be the best choice for a young woman, in the next chapter.) I was in a hurry to catch up to what it seemed like everyone else was doing and see what all the fuss was about.

WHAT ARE THEY THINKING?

It's hard to know what guys are thinking about, or how they feel about you, even if you ask. Males and females are wired differently: Females use about 30,000 words a day while males may use only 10,000 or so.

One of the frustrating situations with guys is when they stop calling you or lose interest suddenly, just when things seem to be going well. You can rationalize it, analyze it, text them incessantly... or just accept it. Guys don't need our help; if they're interested in us, they'll find a way to get our attention. There's no need to exhaust your energy chasing them. Any guy who wants you and doesn't want to work for your affections is a waste of time anyway.

Another thing not worth stressing about is when guys sabotage a perfectly good relationship. The reason? They could have self-esteem issues and not feel worthy of being loved by a good woman, as I experienced first-hand with my former husband, when we were first dating. You just have to make a choice and decide if you'll continue to love and stay with a person who's not treating you the way you deserve to be treated. Decide what you want for yourself, command respect, and when guys see how you carry yourself, they'll either treat you better or hit the road. When you love yourself, it shows, and it separates the men from the boys and the women from the girls.

PLEASE DON'T BELIEVE IT!
Are you falling for the sweet talk that guys feed you?

> *Girls, you know you better watch out*
> *some guys, some guys are only about*
> *that thing, that thing, that thing*
> *that thing, that thing, that thing*
> —Lauryn Hill, "Doo Wop (That Thing)"

Sometimes people say things that they don't really mean when they're mad. You internalize the words, take them personally, and dwell on it, even if you forgive them later. Well, the same goes for "pillow talk"—conversations two people have just before or after having sex. Beware that this is prime territory for some sweet talk, or validation that you are pretty or desirable. You really don't know what to believe—especially if you don't know the person well. But sometimes you say things you don't mean—and believe things you hear—just because you're in that moment of intimacy, even though it may be false intimacy. (I hope this kind of talk doesn't sound too familiar to you. If so, be sure to read on for ways to deal with the situation. If not, you may also benefit from reading on, to avoid falling for such false talk. You can read more on this and other issues regarding sex in the next chapter.)

I fell for a lot of these pillow-talk conversations with my second boyfriend, Kevin, with whom I had a long-distance relationship. At the time, he was 20 and I was 18. One day when Kevin and I were just holding each other after sex, he said: "I care about you so much it's not even funny. I hate it when you leave. When you're not with me, I think about you all the time, and when you're with me all I wanna do is hold you... so I guess you could say I love you, too. All I wanna do is be with you. That's why I'm out here hustling [he was a drug-dealer], because I want to be able to give you anything you need, so you won't have to ask because I'll have it to give to you, but I don't want to tell you, I want to show you. I want to prove it to you. I see you in my future. Can you see me in your future?"

Sweet Talk

Why do so many females fall for the sweet talk that guys feed them? Could it be because they:

- Don't want to lose a guy's attention and/or approval
- Care more about the guy's opinion of them than their own values
- Think they're in love
- Heard him say "I love you"
- Don't want to be teased by their friends
- Need reassurance and validation that they're pretty, special, and desirable
- See and hear prevalent sexuality in movies and music videos
- Feel like everyone else is doing it
- Haven't set up personal boundaries
- Are in some kind of trouble and need "rescuing"

I agreed that I wanted to live with him and always be with him. Then he said, "Everything I do, I do it for you." I paused momentarily, then said, "I don't know what to say... are you sure you won't get tired of me?" and he said, "I'm sure. I'm yours forever. I'll never leave you." Then I asked if he'd do something for me: Walk with me to get my prescription. He said, "Only if you hold my hand all the way." The prescription was for the STD that I caught because he was cheating! Crazy, but I believed every word he said that night.

In another pillow-talk conversation, he said no one else had ever made him feel the way I did, and that I had his heart, so he was therefore vulnerable and I could hurt him; that someday I would be his wife before long "if the money's right." He asked me if I still loved him because he needed assurance. He also told me to forget my parents because he was going to take care of me, so that I wouldn't need or want for anything. He said he had a lot invested in our relationship, that I made him very happy, and that he still couldn't believe I was his. He said I was the most beautiful girl he had ever, or would ever see, even when I woke up with my hair all wild and messed up—I was always beautiful to him. We agreed that our relationship wasn't based on sex (we were kidding ourselves). He also said that his ex-girlfriend (with whom my friend Angela caught him cheating while we were in different cities) is a cool person, but she was in the past permanently. She told him he'd always be hers, but he said there was only one girl for him (me). He said he'd tell the world he loved me. It is sickening to me writing this, all these years later... but you get the point: all talk, no substance.

So don't take it to heart when a guy says he'll stay with you forever. Most of them won't. In the previous examples, I suspect he was telling me this because our relationship was new, or because he felt some strong emotions in the "afterglow" of sex. Forever is a long time. If you are blessed to unite with a man who becomes your husband, that can be forever; though it's not for everyone.

Why did I believe what he was saying? Because I was always looking for someone to connect with—who accepted me and loved me—but the problem was, I didn't really love myself. And I didn't have a relationship with the one who matters the most—God. Even though I accepted Jesus as my personal Savior at age 10, I didn't build a personal relationship with Him until I was well into adulthood.

You can't fill a void in your heart with a guy, sex, food, money, drugs, alcohol, or anything else in this world—all these things are just temporary fixes that leave you feeling empty when you abuse them. The only way to satisfy the void in your soul is by having and maintaining a personal relationship with Jesus Christ. I'll talk about this more in Chapter 14, "What's Wrong With Church?"

> **The only way to satisfy the void in your soul is by having and maintaining a personal relationship with Jesus Christ.**

TO THE RESCUE? SAVE YOURSELF INSTEAD

I remember the summer when Kevin's best friends got evicted, and his mother moved, leaving Kevin without a place to stay as well. Kevin's friends said they wanted to move into my apartment (90 miles away)... Of course, I didn't believe them; but they tried. Kevin's sister told me not to let his friends in my house, because I'd have "a house full of niggas" and they wouldn't work if they knew I was paying the rent. She told me, "Never rescue a man."

Kevin also had his share of jail time, since he sold drugs. I remember taking a $1,000 cash advance from a credit card to pay a bail bondsman for him and wiring it to one of his best friends. I was going to college full time, and making less than $6 per hour at my part-time job. Kevin told me that he'd repay me once he had some money for himself. Of course, he never did. I chalked it up as a loss.

Early in my relationship with my former husband Mike, he got a warrant from the IRS for a business he never owned. I told him I could pay his rent and other living expenses until his $2,000 fine was paid off.

Why do females offer to pay for things that essentially rescue males from themselves? When you rescue someone, they don't have to learn from their mistakes or face consequences for their careless actions. Mike was eight years older than me. He was perfectly capable of taking care of himself before I came on the scene. I heeded Kevin's sister's advice and stood my ground, not giving in to the pressure to rent an apartment for a bunch of dudes to live in and mooch off of me. Instead, I got an apartment and lived by myself for awhile before moving back in with my parents and finishing college.

Like Kevin's sister said, don't ever rescue a man.

GETTING HIT UP

I remember how guys in high school used to go around slapping girls' butts. My own cousin did it to me before we knew we were cousins. I hated it! I'd shriek or tell them to stop, but they thought it was funny, and no girl was safe. I remember one day, I was coming down the stairs when another guy slapped my butt and I turned around and smacked him in the head really hard. He got mad and said, "Girl, if you ever do that again, you'll be pickin' up teeth off the floor." But it was an empty threat—he never touched me again.

I've been in relationships that were emotionally and/or verbally abusive, but not physically abusive. However, they're all bad, and I can't say that any one is worse than the others. Unfortunately, I've had elements of domestic violence in two relationships in particular. They were isolated incidents, and I can't say for sure what I would have done if they had escalated or become repetitive. What I can tell you is there is absolutely no justification for someone to hit you. If you put your hands on him first, you're guilty of provoking him, but even in that case, he only needs to defend himself or walk away--he never has a right to attack you.

Don't ever let anyone try to justify hitting you. There is never a good reason.

The day I broke up with my first boyfriend, Steve, was because of such an incident. One day he made me very angry for teasing me nonstop. We were in his room at his mother's house, and he was going on and on, irritating me and getting the best of me. I lost my temper and I kicked him in the shoulder, and he immediately punched me in my bare leg (it was summertime and I was wearing shorts) and made me leave. He wouldn't speak to me on the phone for a while, and we never got back together.

Fast forward about six months. That's when I saw him at a new club when I was visiting home from college one weekend. I couldn't believe it when he kept coming up to me, dancing with me and saying, "You know you're my old booty," trying to be funny as usual. He said he regretted beating me up that night and wished it never happened. He complimented me on my hair, saying I changed up and that I looked good (it was short and blonde because I was going through the Mary J. and Faith phase in the late '90s). We talked a bit more, and I gave him my pager number so we could hook up while I was home. But after we broke up, I didn't have much connection with him. He said he didn't like the new Daree because I had changed (read: I had moved on).

That one incident is the only time Steve tried to hurt me with his hands, but the temper of my former husband was much worse. Mike explained that he was always ready to destroy something in his house when he got mad at me. He told me he wasn't stable, because he's this way one day and that way the next, which was true. (Little did I know that he had mental issues that precluded him from becoming emotionally stable. He has bipolar disorder and refused to seek professional assistance or treatment.) At various times, I remember him throwing telephones at the walls (damaging them), tossing a couch in my direction, kicking and destroying a new coffee table, and even throwing me on the floor once. All these incidents were spaced out over years, during arguments when I was usually yelling and swearing at him, which didn't help those situations a bit. Again, provocation is no excuse.

During our first summer together, we took a trip for me to meet his family for July 4th weekend. I don't remember what we were arguing about, but I lost my temper, smacked Mike, and ripped off his chain. For hours afterward, he drove us around New York City while giving me the silent treatment. No matter what I said for the rest of the day, he wouldn't respond. The next morning, he packed my things from his apartment and brought them to my house and put them on the front porch.

When my mom called, she wanted to know what was going on. I told her all the cruel things Mike said to me about it "being over." She said, "People say things they don't mean when they're mad, but if he loves you like he says he does, it will work itself out no matter what he said." I was afraid of losing Mike because it seemed like he was all I had. At that point, I didn't deal with my girlfriends anymore. It had been all about Mike, 24/7, for months. It was my fault for building my world around him. I didn't have balance. In any case, he eventually forgave me (you'll learn more about what happened with Mike in Chapter 10, "What's Wrong With Getting Married"). I just want to be clear that physical violence is wrong regardless of who "started it."

Speaking of women provoking fights, as I write this, the publicity over the infamous beat down between Chris Brown and Rihanna has cooled down. Rihanna decided not to take him back, as she told Diane Sawyer on *Dateline* because she didn't want any of her fans to think it was OK to go back to an abuser. She understands that many girls look up to her and she didn't want to send the wrong message. If you're in a situation where your boyfriend, parent, or anyone else is abusing you, you do have a way out. Call the SAFE national hotline toll free at (800) 799-SAFE and talk to a trained professional who's there to listen and advise you how to get help.

Too many people have died needlessly at the hands of an abuser (or have become so depressed they committed suicide), even when others knew about it or suspected the abusive behavior. If you know a girl who needs to get to safety, don't hesitate to call on her behalf. You are your sister's keeper. Don't look the other way—it could be a matter of life and death.

**You are your sister's keeper.
Don't look the other way.**

MR. RIGHT?

We all want to be desired, touched and loved—that's how God made us. We all want to spend time with a special person in our lives, and feel needed and wanted. But we have to be respected first. Who will respect you if you don't respect yourself? A guy who only makes room in his life to have sex with you is not the one for you. A guy who is worthy of you will take the time to know you and love you first.

And don't fall for the trap of thinking that a man is fair game if he's separated, even if he has the legal papers to prove it. Either you're married or you're single—you can't be both married and single at the same time. If he hasn't gotten divorced yet, there's a reason, and until then, he's off limits. Regardless of his intentions, don't get entangled in his mess. Start off fresh with someone who has a clean slate and is emotionally available.

A relationship is only as good as whatever both parties bring to it. If someone tells you, "I don't believe in religion, but I'm spiritual," find out exactly what that means to him. To many people, religion equals rules. We do need to have some rules to maintain order in this world, right? We can't all decide to live however and do whatever we please without any rules, constraints or consequences. (Take the universal law of gravity. If you throw something up, it's not going to stay there for long.) It's dangerous to be led by a man who's in a spiritual wilderness. Don't think you can pull up a guy—it's not your job. Stay single if that's your only alternative. If he says he's a Christian, yet his character or lifestyle doesn't reflect Christian values—don't connect with him, not even to establish a friendship (especially if an attraction exists). Run!

A relationship is only as good as whatever both parties bring to it.

When you do contemplate a relationship, make sure you're equally grounded in your religious beliefs, money habits, and goals in life. You will always have issues with a guy who does not share or support your values and goals.

Many guys your age (and in their 20s and 30s, too) are unsure of where they're going in life. They may not have worked out their goals or may still just not be ready to settle down. But if you choose to date someone seriously and want to have a healthy relationship, here are some attributes you should look for to make sure he's the "Right One":

- He takes the initiative to show that he wants you and invests time in courting you.
- He doesn't make plans that he never backs up.
- He doesn't play games or send confusing messages (he says what he means and means what he says).
- He backs up his words with action.
- He has good friends, and you like how he acts when he's around them.
- He's willing to learn from his mistakes and modify his actions accordingly.
- He doesn't try to control you.

⊚ He's grateful for what you offer and give to him.
He appreciates you.

⊚ He communicates with you.

⊚ He doesn't abuse or mistreat you.

CONSIDER THIS

You have to be whole, before you can be in a good relationship. Another person can compliment you, but not complete you—it's God's job to fill your void. Before you can expect others to treat you well, you have to respect yourself and treat yourself well. Set the standard for what you want from your colleagues, friends, lovers, and family members.

When you have low self-esteem, you look for your worth in others. You want to be with someone who makes you feel good about yourself and "approves" of you. That's why we often make compromises to engage in sex, because we think it's a fast track to intimacy, acceptance, and love. But that couldn't be further from the truth. Looking for validation in the wrong places will only leave you disappointed and (still) empty inside. When you're empty and you have sex, you're trying to fill a void with false intimacy, which makes it that much worse if the relationship falls apart or the guy abandons you. Respect yourself and don't give your body to just anyone. Guard your heart and save it for someone worthy of it.

**When you're empty and
you have sex, you're trying to fill
a void with false intimacy.**

It's up to you to command respect from the opposite sex by first respecting yourself. How do you dress and present yourself in public? What kind of clothing do you wear to school or work? (Remember what we discussed in Chapter 2, "What's Wrong With My Looks?") How do you speak to others, and how do you carry yourself? In your normal conversation, do you refer to yourself or other females as b*tches, chicks, or ladies? Despite contemporary notions, the word "b*tch" is not an empowering word, any more than is the word "nigga" (whether it has an "a" or an "er" on the end)!

Do you think highly of yourself and know your worth, or are you just relieved if anyone gives you special attention? Chances are, a guy won't treat you better than you treat yourself. From here on, let a guy pursue you—you don't do the chasing. Instead of giving your heart and body to him, present an air of mystery and modesty (in other words, cover up your goods), and let him win you over. He needs to prove himself—and you're worth it!

FURTHER READING

Christian psychologists Henry Cloud and John Townsend have written several books about establishing healthy boundaries, including *Boundaries in Dating: Making Dating Work*. Shannon Ethridge goes even deeper with *Every Young Woman's Battle: Guarding Your Mind, Heart, and Body in a Sex-Saturated World*, which will make you think about what you're doing before you "do it." Read both of these resources and arm yourself with the defenses you need to protect your body and your heart in romantic relationships.

8

WHAT'S **WRONG** with sex?

"Someone asked me, 'Why is it such a big deal to wait to have sex until you get married? Why not test drive the car before you buy it?' The test drive never ends; in your soul, in your mind, you take the ride with you to the next car, and the miles keep adding up."

— **KIRK FRANKLIN** —

I once heard (during a sermon!) that single people are mad because they can't have sex, and married people are mad because they have to (let that sink in). Another pastor I knew put it a different way: "We need to get the married folks back in the bedroom and keep the single folks out [of the bedroom]." So yes, we're going there.

This is the chapter where I talk about guys and sex. I hope you didn't skip the preceding chapters—you should have the foundation of knowing yourself and loving yourself before you can get intimately involved with another person. You should also have a strong network of family and friends to support you as you face the questions that will come along as you deal with romantic situations.

> ### Know and love yourself
> ### *before* you get intimately
> ### involved with another person.

WHY HAVE SEX YOUNG?

I used to be teased about being a virgin. On our first family summer vacation to the Boston area, I was 14 and we stayed with friends of my mother. The friend's niece, Portia, was staying with them, and she was 16. One day, we were walking around in Roxbury, a suburb of Boston, and Portia ran into some dudes she knew in the projects. They asked me if I was a virgin, and when I confirmed it, one of them said, "You don't know what you're missing." Indignant, I told him that at my age, I didn't need to know. Sex wasn't something I was even curious about then, so his comment annoyed me. Why would I choose to have sex so young? What would I get out of it?

Another time in high school, a guy named Tony asked me if I was a virgin. I told him yes, and he said, "Why, because you haven't met the right person yet?" Then his friend Sam asked me, "Are you saving yourself for marriage?"

I told them, "A little bit of both." So then Sam said, "You would like it." I hoped that the third degree was over, but it wasn't. He then made up another question to see what I would do. He said, "Say you're with a boy, and you're all sweaty and kissing and your hormones (at the sound of the word "hormones," he and Tony exchanged a smile) are going and stuff, and then he pulls down your pants, what would you do?" I won't bore you with the rest of the conversation, but I can tell you that they didn't catch me.

I disappointed them both by saying, "It depends on the situation." But Tony did have one good point. If your hormones are going and your defenses are down, you might do it anyway.

TAKING SEX OFF THE TABLE

Songs, music videos, and people everywhere in American culture talk about and refer to sex every day. It seems like sex or sexual innuendo is all around us, whether implicit or explicit. It's easy to think that everybody's doing it, and to be curious about "the do" if you haven't done it.

The morning after I lost my virginity, I remember wondering why sex was such a big deal. It hurt, and I got absolutely no pleasure from it. But as I continued to have sex with my first boyfriend, it hurt less, and I continued to do it, even though I always felt guilty afterward. Looking back now, I wish I had waited before I carelessly gave away my virginity. Back then, I didn't like the feeling of being the only one in my crew who hadn't "done it." I remember in 11th grade when my friend Nette sarcastically asked me if I was waiting for "The One." But there's nothing wrong with waiting.

> ### There's nothing wrong with waiting to have sex.

The person you see at face value isn't always the real person. If you want to find out whether a guy you're dating really likes you, spend a lot of time with him, in various environments (with his friends, family, and yours), and take sex off the table. When you don't have sex with him, you'll see him for who he is, and you'll stay more objective and protect your heart in the process.

OK, THIS IS AWKWARD!

Having sex with a person for the first time is very nerve-wracking—especially if you believe like I do, that premarital sex is wrong. You have a lot of insecurities, and you hope that the guy will still like you afterward.

Steve was patient with me when I gave him my virginity. (At that time, I was the third girl who had done so!) The first time, I felt extremely vulnerable, nervous, and uncomfortable. I told him I was afraid that he would leave me after it was over, but I felt like I had gone too far to turn back. What I didn't know is that guys can also feel stress and pressure when it comes to sex.

The second guy that I had sex with was a college classmate. We were both in long-distance relationships, but that didn't stop us from having a fling. One of the things he told me to reassure me before our first time was that first of all, I couldn't disappoint him, and second, girls can't be disappointing anyway because all the pressure is on the guy. I didn't buy that. Then I started telling him about my insecurities with my body. He said, "No one that's afraid to be naked is ready to have sex," and that no one's body is perfect, but so what? Again, these objections did not stop us from proceeding. I was 18 then, but I still had no business having sex with him because it went against my personal values:

- ๛ I was too young
- ๛ I didn't believe in premarital sex
- ๛ I had a boyfriend (although I probably didn't care then because I had just learned that he had knocked up an underage girl while I was away)
- ๛ He had a girlfriend

I wasn't proud of being "the other woman," and unfortunately that wasn't the last time (I'll tell you more about that later in Chapter 10, "What's Wrong With Getting Married?").

SAVED AND HAVING SEX

I was raised in church, and no matter which church I've attended, I rarely ever heard anything about sex from the pulpit. I grew up as a Christian, being taught that fornication (an unmarried person having sex) and adultery (a married person having sex with someone they're not married to) were sins. And that's pretty much what I got from "the talk" with my mother, somewhere around the 5th grade (All she said was: "It's wrong. Don't do it.").

I believe God established these rules for our protection, so we can avoid a lot of pain and heartache. But neither the fear of God nor of my parents stopped me from having sex.

I remember going on a women's trip with my church when I was married (our church called it the "Women's Advance" instead of a retreat). We went to the Poconos area of Pennsylvania, and I shared a room with an older woman who was single, really cool, and had a daughter close to my age. The woman told me that she and her man were having sex, and that she loves sex. I asked her if she ever prayed about it, and she said, "Yeah, I prayed about it, and God said it was OK. My man is OK with it, too." I bet he was... but He wasn't.

Make no mistake — God will never tell you to do something that contradicts his Word:

"Do you not know that the wicked will not inherit the kingdom of God? Do not be deceived: Neither the sexually immoral nor idolaters nor adulterers nor male prostitutes nor homosexual offenders nor thieves nor the greedy nor drunkards nor slanderers nor swindlers will inherit the kingdom of God."
(1 Corinthians 6:9-10 NIV)

God is not a man that He should lie. I knew back then, listening to her story, that sex outside of marriage was not

OK with God, but I didn't challenge her. Plus, since I was married at the time, fornication wasn't something I was struggling with anymore.

OTHER REASONS TO KEEP YOUR "V-CARD"

Do you feel like you're missing something if you don't have sex? You are — pregnancy, suicide, depression, and poverty, to name a few. It may feel like everybody's doing it, but they're not. A vast majority of teens graduate from high school as virgins, like I did, and it's nothing to be ashamed of. Having sex too soon, with the wrong person, or for the wrong reasons has painful consequences at any age. A lot of people don't think ahead and consider the effects that their actions today will have on them in the future.

Stop and think about how your actions today will affect your future.

Just as getting pregnant won't keep a guy from leaving you, having sex with a guy won't make him like you more, and it certainly won't make him love you or stay in a relationship with you (if you're in one). In his book *Letters to a Young Sister*, actor, author, and activist Hill Harper says that some guys have such low self-esteem and think so little of them-selves, that they think even less of you if you allow them to "hit it." And, of course, whenever rape or sexual assault is involved, they don't think much of you at all. There's a total lack of respect. That's why it's so important for you to have yourself together mentally and spiritually before you decide to give your heart, body, and soul to another person. You also need to be emotionally mature enough to deal with the consequences.

You to have to be mentally and spiritually ready to give your heart, body, and soul to another person.

If being hurt by a guy, getting pregnant, or disappointing God doesn't make you cautious about sex, then sexually transmitted diseases (STDs) should.

I've contracted HPV (otherwise known as genital warts), trichomoniasis, and chlamydia at different times from different guys. I thank God that I recognized the symptoms and was able to have them treated and cured. If you get treated for an STD, you should take all the medicine, even if you start feeling better after a couple of days, and your partner should also be treated. Otherwise, if you continue having sex with each other and only one of you has finished taking the medicine, you run the risk of getting reinfected. Everything that anyone your partner has had sex with can potentially get passed on to you. Untreated STDs can cause fertility problems and even death. Do you really want to go through the stress and discomfort of having an STD and getting the medication to stop the unpleasant side effects?

Not enough people use condoms to protect themselves from STDs. Not enough people discuss birth control or their sexual history with their sexual partners. Too often, people assume that the other person is "good" because of their appearance (they don't look sick), so there's nothing to worry about. Not so fast. As much as I hate to hear about unplanned pregnancies, I really hate to hear about all the new cases of AIDS, HIV, and other STDs.

The Centers for Disease Control and Prevention (CDC) show that STDs are higher than ever among teens. In 2010 they estimated 19 million new sexually transmitted infections occur each year, almost half among 15- to 24-year-olds, including AIDS (39 percent). More than 400,000 U.S. teen girls ages 15-19 were infected with chlamydia and gonorrhea, but HPV is the most common sexually transmitted infection in teen girls aged 14 to 19, while the highest overall prevalence is among Black girls (nearly half the Blacks studied had at least one STD). That rate compared with 20 percent among both whites and Mexican-American teens.

Apparently, these teens are having unprotected sex and may not realize that you can get STDs from oral, vaginal, or anal sex.

For All the Wrong Reasons

The idea of having sex always starts with a thought. Second-guessing. Wondering. What-ifs. Certain situations loosen boundaries and make us more vulnerable to premarital sex, and one too many compromises will make it all the easier for us to engage in it:

- Wearing suggestive, revealing clothing (too short, too tight, or low-cut), either in person or in online pictures
- Sexting
- Exposing yourself to crude, suggestive media and images (TV, movies, and songs)
- The (false) notion that oral sex and masturbation don't count as sex

You can do any or all of the above to get a guy's attention, but these methods won't keep it for long once he puts all his clothes back on.

MOUTH DOESN'T COUNT?

One day when I was in the fifth grade, I was walking home with two of my friends. They started talking secretively about something, and I was feeling a little left out. When I tried to get in the conversation, they asked me if I knew what a blow job was. I didn't, but when I think about it now, I was about 10 years old, and none of us should have known what that meant. But they gave each other a look and left me in the dark. I went home upset and asked my 16-year-old brother about it since the girls wouldn't tell me. He said I was too young. Then my mom heard the fuss, took me aside and showed me the dictionary definition of "whore" but still didn't explain the term "blow job."

If you're not married to the person you're having sex with, you're sinning—no way around it.

Don't let anyone deceive you into thinking that oral sex is safer or better than regular (vaginal) sexual intercourse because you can't get pregnant. You can still contract STDs this way. And from a biblical perspective, anything you do with your sexual organs for sexual pleasure is still sex. You can try to get technical and debate about whether oral sex, masturbation, and other sexual activities are sins, but if there's one thing I know the Bible is clear on, it's sexual immorality (see Matthew 5:27-28 and 1 Corinthians 6:12-20). If you're not married to the person you're having sex with, you're sinning, and there's no way around it. Fornication is a sin that can set us apart from God, so we must establish accountability and boundaries in advance.

Setting Boundaries

Make the effort to do some planning before you find yourself in a compromising situation. You can't wait until the butterflies are floating, your hormones are jumping, and your heart is racing to make a rational, logical decision about how far you're willing to go with a guy. Here are some ways to set boundaries on intimacy when you're involved with a guy:

- Avoid alcohol. It impairs your judgment and relaxes your inhibitions.
- Limit the amount of time you spend together alone (whether on the phone or in person).
- Be aware of your exposure to movies, books, and other media that may cause you to feel insecure, discontent, or horny (this is real talk)!
- Get an accountability partner. This should be a person you can trust, who knows where you are and whom you're with. She can keep you in check and make sure you're safe.

**Plan ahead on what
you will do if you find yourself
in a compromising situation.**

SEX IS A DRUG

When you have sex with someone, a hormone called oxytocin is released from your body. Oxytocin is a bonding hormone. This explains why females become so attached to a guy, become less objective, and feel like they're "falling in love" when they're sexually active with a guy repeatedly. But guys don't operate the same way. That's why they can have multiple partners and not feel guilty about it. Females release 100 times more oxytocin than males do.

You can easily lose yourself when you give yourself away. Not to mention, when you have sex with someone, you're also indirectly having sex with everyone that they had sex with—remember, that's how STDs are spread.

Sex can be addictive, and it clouds your judgment. Having sex with someone too soon contributes to attachment not only because of the physical excretion of hormones but also the spiritual exchange, called a "soul tie." God created sex for marriage. If I had set my boundaries and abstained from sex, I would have remained objective, not become emotional, and saw each of these guys for who they really were, without giving up a big part of myself in the process.

> **Sex creates a soul tie between you and your partner, and soul ties are hard to get rid of.**

DAMAGES

People nonchalantly talk about "hooking up" (casual sex) and some girls become pregnant without any fanfare because we're desensitized to it these days, but that doesn't make it right. I remember girls at school who were in 10th grade, pregnant by men (yes, grown men!) in their 20s or 30s! No matter how glamorous or lovely it may seem, or be portrayed in the movies, sex is not a rite of passage for teens, and it's certainly not without consequences. Even if you manage to come through a relationship or promiscuous behavior without catching a disease or becoming pregnant, you'll have to endure and recover from the spiritual and emotional damage. If you decide to have an abortion, you may feel lots of guilt and may need therapy to fully recover from it. If the guy you're having relations with breaks up with you, you will have to deal with the abandonment. There are all sorts of possible consequences that you can avoid by simply keeping your legs closed.

I like the way gospel singer Kelly Chapman put it in her book, *Real: The Truth About Being Single*: "Someone trying to put the eight ball in his pocket without first making a covenant vow [of marriage] is no more than a petty thief. And if we let the thief in and allow him to take all the treasure without him having the right to do so, we become an accomplice." Do you see that? When you willingly have sex with someone, not only are you sinning against your own body, but you're helping them to do so!

God doesn't want us to get hurt, and that's why His Word speaks against premarital sex. It can destroy hearts and cause irreparable damage. Having sex outside of marriage (this includes masturbation) is a sin against your own body and causes a loss of fellowship with God (He will not condone sin). I have always known that, but I haven't always lived by it. And when I didn't abstain from sex as a young, single woman (both before my marriage to Mike and after our divorce), I always regretted it. Take it from me, the emotional and spiritual damage is crushing, especially when you're young.

CONSIDER THIS

Pleasing God often requires sacrifices, but if you decide to make God the Lord of your life and serve Him, He will make it all worthwhile. You may not enjoy delaying gratification and exerting self-control in the moment, but you won't regret it.

Abstinence is easier said than done. Believe me, I know. I wish I could give you some magical way to get around this, but the truth is, it doesn't get any easier. It's rare to see people in the mainstream culture like Pepa (one-third of the pioneer female hip-hop group Salt-N-Pepa), who has, at this writing, maintained celibacy for five years by choice! (If you want to read a great story about overcoming sexual abuse and domestic violence, along with the fascination of her rise as a star, read her memoir, *Let's Talk About Pep*. She explains why she decided to stop having sex at the end of the book.)

We all have the God-given desires to connect intimately with someone else. To keep the enemy at bay, you have to establish boundaries, overcome your fears of what others may think of you, and become more assertive. Waiting can be lonely, and you may be teased about it, but using self-control and surrounding yourself with like-minded, positive people and activities now beats trying to recover from self-destruction later.

For every action, there is a reaction.

It's OK to be a virgin and it's OK to say no, even if it seems like everyone else is doing it. We all have an inner voice, whether you want to refer to it as your gut feeling, conscience, intuition, or God's voice through the Holy Spirit. Listen to that voice when it tells you something isn't quite right before you make a decision that you can't undo. Regret is hard to live with. You can't change the past; so before you engage in a sexual act, think about your future. For every action, there is a reaction. What will be the consequences? Look around your community and you'll likely see examples of how you don't want to end up.

What if you already have regrets about your past? What if you feel bad because you are no longer a virgin and have had sexual encounters (whether they were consensual or forced on you against your will)? You can start with today—it's not too late. Start by saying yes to yourself, and no to whatever makes you unhappy or uncomfortable about having sex. You can always say no, and you can always change your mind, change your path, and decide to do things differently for here on out. God gives us second, third, fourth, and one millionth chances to get things right. He will cleanse you from all your impurities if you ask Him to. God loves us unconditionally. He isn't as harsh of a judge as other people are on us, or as harsh as we are on ourselves. He forgives us when we confess our shortcomings to Him. He also gives us the power to change and make wiser choices next time.

> **God gives us second, third, fourth, and one millionth chances to get things right.**

If you didn't get this at home, it's OK. I'm here to tell you that God loves you, and you need to love you, too. If you don't love yourself, you'll be on a long, never-ending search trying to get that love from others. Read scripture, pray, and learn what gifts God has given you. Take part in confidence-building activities (community groups, ministries at church, and service teams, etc.), and spend time with friends and people who really care about your well-being, and support your endeavors. Be purposeful and give back. Volunteer or serve as a tutor, coach, mentor, or other capacity of service that makes you feel good. And while you're helping someone else, you will actually benefit as well.

FURTHER READING
I've talked a lot about sex and abstinence in
this chapter, but I'm not an expert. I highly recommend
you also read *The Naked Truth: About Sex, Love and
Relationships* by Lakita Garth, *Seductive Delusions:
Exposing Lies About Sex* by Gerard Henry, and *Single, Saved,
and Having Sex* by Ty Adams for more on this subject.

part three

CHECKING IN—WHAT'S YOUR STATUS?

WHAT'S **WRONG** with being single?

"Everyone should nurture their sense of singleness; it will keep them a free person."

— **JERUSHA STEWART** —

*B*eing single isn't a bad thing. You don't need a boyfriend or a husband to be somebody. As I write this, I haven't had a long-term relationship in over five years. During this time, I've talked to men as friends, and dated here and there, but not one of them was truly a match for us to have a relationship. I'll talk about why in a moment.

Statistics show that women of all races are staying single longer these days than ever before. In 2009, 51 percent of American women were unmarried, as were 51 percent of Latina women, 45 percent of non-Hispanic White women, and 41 percent of Asian women.[3]

SO WHY ARE YOU SINGLE?

Let's get this term "single" straight. Not everyone defines it the same way, and some reject it because of their own views (they may be in a gay partnership or widowed, etc.). However, for the purposes of this book, I define "single" to mean not currently married. If you're separated, you're still married. If you're not married (widowed, divorced, never been married, or just have a boyfriend/girlfriend/live-in partner), then you're single.

I've grown beyond tired of being asked why I'm single. Sometimes it's stated a little differently: "If you're single, then there must be something wrong with you." Is that right? What—a successful, attractive, intelligent female can't be single unless something is wrong with her?

You don't have to have a boyfriend or a husband to be somebody.

Singleness is often a conscious choice. I don't know many people who enjoy dating overall because of the uncertainty, the games, insecurities and issues we have to sort through—both with ourselves and when getting to know someone new. Who wants to share a miniature version of their life story and get to know someone only to have to repeat the whole cycle a few months later with someone else? But here I am, single again after my divorce. And the dating game is still no fun.

I've received so much rejection in this area that I spent some time thinking that something must be wrong with me because I'm the common denominator in my dating life. I often wanted to be treated a certain way, but then lowered my standards temporarily, and settled for what I thought I could get instead of what I was worth.

I settled for what I could get instead of what I was worth.

You teach people how to treat you. I know that I'm smart, attractive, social, ambitious, and God-fearing. But the men I have met have been too busy to give me attention, only wanted sex without a commitment, just wanted to keep me on the side, had incompatible personalities or character qualities I couldn't tolerate for long, or it was none of the above, but just bad timing. I can't ignore any of those things because they'll remain present—you can't change another person.

Sometimes personalities don't click. Sometimes there's no chemistry or mutual physical attraction. Sometimes I think I'm ready for a relationship, but the guy isn't (because of emotional/financial/spiritual circumstances that are in conflict with mine).

I'm sure these guys had reasons for letting me go as well, but I think it's better to be miserable while you're alone than to get help being miserable (hence the ubiquitous phrase, "I can do bad all by myself"). But who says you have to be miserable at all being single? I'm doing pretty well by myself, thank you! I've gone back and forth with my attitude about singleness and my overall sense of contentment before accepting my status. I know there are pros and cons about being single and being married, and I've experienced both. Don't rush to get into a relationship!

ALONE ≠ LONELY

Are you an introvert or an extrovert? I get my energy at times from others (extroverted) and at times from being alone (introverted). I like the quiet and being alone with my thoughts. I don't know why people are afraid to be alone.

You can learn to enjoy the silence of your own company. I remember the days when I needed music bumpin' or the TV blaring constantly in the background because I was so uncomfortable with the silence. I was running from my inner voice, trying to drown me out. Nowadays, I'm comfortable with silence and find that when my inner me speaks, I need to listen. Looking back over things, I have a few regrets and can track notable moments when I should have just said no. All these moments have one thing in common: I wasn't listening to myself, not honoring what "she" had to say.

JUST SAY NO

Do you have a hard time saying 'No' to certain people when they ask you for money or other favors? As financial guru Suze Orman says, "Say no [to loved ones] out of love for yourself, instead of saying yes out of fear." This goes for toxic family and friends, people misusing you, and so on. If they reject you because you don't give them what they want (let them borrow money, do a favor, or whatever the case may be), it's OK. They'll live and the world won't stop spinning. As renowned evangelist, author, and host of the show Enjoying Everyday Life Joyce Meyer says, "You don't need a wishbone, you need a backbone." If you don't stand up for yourself, no one else will!

CONSIDER THIS

Being single is just one of many attributes we may have. But while the word "single" may describe you, it doesn't define you. Being single means being separate, unique, and whole. When you're single, you can take the time to find out who you are, what you like, what you need, and what makes you tick. You can have a rich, satisfying life of freedom when you're single. You don't have to coordinate your schedule with his or ask his opinion about activities. Conversely, when you're in a relationship or married, your attention is divided, so you're always balancing your wants and needs with your mate's. And if you're a parent, the balancing act gets even more interesting—and challenging.

You shape and mold your children as you raise them, but your mate is already set as the person he is. You cannot raise a man. So the attention demanded from you as a girlfriend or wife is very different from that of a mom.

My advice is not to make getting married your number-one goal. You have a lot of latitude when you're a single female, and God will honor your commitment to Him.

So get comfortable in your own skin. Get to know what you want and what you like by being still sometimes. Listen to the quietness. Spend some time alone with yourself—don't be afraid to go to a movie or get a spa service on your own. Treat yourself. If you don't love yourself, who will?

FURTHER READING

Singleness is not a curse—embrace it! Ideas from mogul Kimora Lee Simmons' *Fabulosity: What it Is and How to Get It* **and Ebony magazine Editor-in-Chief Amy Dubois Barnett's** *Get Yours! How to Have Everything You've Ever Dreamed of and More* **will show you how.**

10

WHAT'S **WRONG** with getting married?

"A husband cannot say, 'I'll love my wife after she starts respecting me,' and a wife cannot say, 'I'll love my husband after he starts loving me.' Each spouse must exhibit unconditional love and respect for the other."

— **EMERSON EGGERICHS** —

Marriage isn't for everybody. We may think the grass is greener on the other side—single people want to get married and have a committed partner, while married people sometimes wish they had the freedom that the single life brings. I can relate to both, since I'm divorced. Because I've experienced both sides—and it wasn't all good—most of my advice in this chapter comes from the perspective of what *not* to do.

BREAKUPS TO MAKEUPS

I met my former husband Mike at the nursing home where we both worked as certified nursing assistants (CNAs). At the time, I was 20 years old, living with my parents and attending college full time to finish my bachelor's degree. I didn't even like him "that way" at first, so I had no idea he would ever "put a ring on it."

Mike was eight years older than I and he lived within walking distance of the nursing home, as did I (but in the opposite direction). We worked the same shift, and since neither of us had a car, we both walked to and from work (sometimes together if I spent the night at his place). Our dating relationship was on and off for two years before we got married. Our biggest breakup was just a few days before I graduated. Shortly thereafter, he moved to a different part of the state (near New York City), and I moved in with my brother in Baltimore.

I was upset that Mike didn't come to my graduation. In spite of our issues, I thought he would want to celebrate that milestone occasion with me. He knew how hard I worked, how smart I was, and how driven I was. I had even helped him with his homework sometimes so he could earn his general equivalency diploma (GED). But Mike didn't show. My whole day had a depressing cloud over it without him there to celebrate with me. I'll never forget that. I didn't know if I would ever see him again.

I made a list of reasons why I was better off without him (his debts and bad credit, lack of education, low self-esteem, indecisiveness, reluctance to relocate with me, and untrustworthiness). Then I thought about why I still wanted to be with him (the familiarity, closeness and intimacy, friendship, love, sincere caring). The positives truly didn't outweigh the negatives, but I listened to my heart instead of my head. I had never lived in a big city before, and I thought I needed him to start my new life because I wasn't confident. I didn't want to start all over in a new relationship with someone else. It's funny because as I write this, I'm single, but I no longer let the thought of not wanting to start over keep me stuck in bad situations.

If you find yourself wondering whether to stay in a relation-ship, make a list of the non-negotiable qualities you want in a mate, pray over it, and then stick to it. Having standards doesn't necessarily mean you're too picky. It's best to be clear about your morals, values, and needs up front. If you fight with someone too often, you're incompatible. Breaking up with someone frequently (as in my on-again, off-again relationship) also means you're incompatible. You can love a guy without being in a relationship with him. End the rela-tionship and move on.

Looking back, I wish I had let Mike go then, but I didn't. Who knows what my life would be like now if I had. My friends tried to console me, saying that I was too good for him, and he didn't deserve me. But it didn't matter what they said to me—what mattered most to me then was what I had in my head, and I really thought I needed him. I thought that because he was eight years older than me, he was wiser than me. But now I know that age and experience doesn't necessarily equal wisdom. To be considered wise, you have to learn from your mistakes and not continually repeat them. Reading a book back then like Dr. Bethany Marshall's *Deal Breakers: When to Work on a Relationship and When to Walk Away* would have opened my eyes.

If you're wise, you eventually learn from your mistakes instead of repeating them.

Unfortunately, I didn't heed the sound advice. Mike and I reunited a few months later. We got engaged, and we moved into our first apartment together just outside Washington,

D.C. Before that move, I had never lived in a large metropolitan area or a predominantly Black area that included all different classes (upper, middle, and low). I thought I needed to be with Mike because he was older and more worldly than I was. I was sheltered and book-smart, while he was more "hood" and street-smart. But in spite of becoming an adult and starting a life together, some of the old stuff that drove us apart remained because our mental states hadn't changed.

HE'S MINE (UNOFFICIALLY)

Mike enlisted in the Army National Guard, and we spent months apart before he came back and married me. But first, he had to get divorced. Yep, Mike was separated from his wife geographically, but not legally, for several years, which included our dating relationship. He told me he didn't get divorced because of the hassle and the money, and that he never thought he would get married again, so why bother? He also didn't know where his wife lived for a long time because they lost touch and moved on with their lives. I told myself it was OK to be involved with him because she wasn't around, and they had no children together. But the truth was, as long as he was separated, he couldn't truly be mine, no matter what he told me or how he felt about me.

Before we got married, Mike's wife called our apartment one day out of the blue. She was living in North Carolina. I don't remember what the holdup was, but I had to postpone the wedding because she took her time signing the divorce papers. I didn't understand why, and he didn't tell me. Another time when he wasn't there, she called and told me the opposite—that Mike was the one holding up the divorce. The sad thing was, I paid for their divorce so we could hurry and get married, even though I wasn't making much money myself then. I felt guilty about living with someone I wasn't married to, let alone someone who was married to someone else. Years later, I also paid for our divorce, which cost much more, and not just in money. (That's an example of something called "stupid tax," which I'll discuss in Chapter 13, "What's Wrong With My Money?")

Although Mike's wife was clearly not in his life, and they didn't even communicate, Mike was still emotionally and spiritually unavailable. I used to sing Carl Thomas' song, "I Wish" full of regret (changing the gender-specific pronouns, of course). The chorus was:

> *I wish I never met her at all,*
> *Even though I love her so*
> *And she got love for me*
> *But she still belongs to someone else.*

It's a huge mistake to get involved with a man who's unavailable. A guy who's married (including those who are separated, legally or not), has a clingy ex-girlfriend, doesn't have time for you, is consumed by his work, or is not available. Staying with someone like that is no different from settling. If you want an intimate emotional and spiritual connection in your relationship, avoid unavailable guys, and save yourself the heartache and frustration. Don't kid yourself into thinking you won't get attached to someone just because you know that logically (and legally), they belong to someone else.

**It's a huge mistake
to get involved with a guy
who's unavailable.**

THE BEGINNING OF THE END

For many years, Mike and I tried not to fight, and to just love and accept each other, but we just couldn't get along. The demise of our dating relationship (multiple times over) was also the demise of our marriage. My strong-willed nature and quick temper didn't help, and his unregulated bipolar disorder was a contributing factor. I thought my way was better than his in many situations, and sometimes I looked down on him. We didn't compromise enough for each other, and we were selfish. Mike also had a temper, and we both said terrible, hateful things to each other that we regret. Even after apologies are said and done, we can't take those words back. It's often easier to forgive than to forget.

> **Be careful what you say.**
> **You can't take back your words.**

I didn't like to compromise, but marriage is all about compromise and submission (for women, biblically speaking), to release your will at times to sacrifice for your mate. In the book *Love and Respect* by Emerson Eggerichs, I learned that males respond well to their innate need for respect, while females have an innate need to be loved. (The scriptural foundation for the book is Ephesians 5:33.)

I knew our marriage was ending in early 2004 when Mike accused me of cheating on him, and I accused him of being a deadbeat husband. He was no stranger to quitting a job if someone at work made him mad, and one of those times was when I was pregnant with our daughter. I, on the other hand, was having an emotional affair, but I didn't admit it at the time. I deceived myself into thinking that it was OK for me to talk on the phone to another man because it was long-distance and nothing physical was going on—we just talked. But I was sharing my innermost feelings with a man other than my estranged husband because it felt emotionally safe—but it wasn't.

I filed the legal separation papers in the summer of 2004, just two months shy of our fifth wedding anniversary, and shortly after moving to Hampton, Virginia, with my daughter and sister. My daughter was 10 months old and had just learned how to walk. I had just received my master's degree. I was truly starting all over in a place where I knew no one. My mother moved in with me a few months later—and she was also about to file for divorce from my dad. Oh yeah, and my brother was getting divorced, too. That was not the best year for my family.

CONSIDER THIS

Some situations are easy to get into, but hard to get out of. I'm not proud of having been engaged to a married man, but I was 22. I've since forgiven myself. I've learned that if a relationship doesn't start out right, it won't end right.

In life we have different seasons where people come and go. Each person that comes into our lives has a purpose, but not each of them need to come into your life and stay there.

Nothing is wrong with wanting to be married or getting married to the right person. I prayed during my relationship, and I remember praying early on the morning of my wedding day—but I never truly listened for the small still voice of God telling me what to do. I didn't wait for God's approval. I didn't want to let go of the mate I wanted, or to allow room for God to bring me the kind of mate I needed. I wanted to have things my way and then try to get God to bless it. But that's not how God works. He wants you to do things His way. Sometimes we get into a mess and want God to get us out of it, but the only way to get out of that kind of mess is to let it go.

**Everything can't be fixed.
Sometimes the only way to get
out of a mess is to let it go.**

Surrender and give up. Give up the frustration, stress, and worry of trying to do things your way, or trying to get others to act right. God will always give you a way out of a situation, even if you don't like His method. You have to put your pride aside and be willing to do the grunt work, and take the steps to move on even if your feelings tell you differently: "The heart is deceitful among all things... Who can understand it?" (Jeremiah 17:9 NIV)

This chapter was one of the least flattering for me to write, but I have to be honest. My goal is not to look perfect, but to be real with you and share what I've learned from being married and divorced. I hope my pain will help you avoid making the same types of mistakes in your life.

FURTHER READING

Depending on your age and perspective, marriage may or may not be something you're wondering about at this point. If you are, and you want to get a biblical perspective on the differing needs of men and women in a marriage, and how to break destructive cycles that could lead to divorce, delve into *Love and Respect* by Emerson Eggerichs. And all types of romantic relationships can benefit from Dr. Bethany Marshall's *Deal Breakers: When to Work on a Relationship and When to Walk Away*.

11

WHAT'S **WRONG** with being a single mom?

> "Making the decision to have a child is momentous. It is to decide forever to have your heart go walking around outside your body."
>
> — **ELIZABETH STONE** —

ingle-parent families are more common now than ever. When I think of all the single parents in America—especially teen mothers—I wonder, why them and not me? As of this writing, I am a single mother, but my experience began in my mid-20s—not my teens. I knew so many girls in my high school who had at least one child (and/or a miscarriage, or an abortion), as early as 13 and 14 years old. And with shows like MTV's *Pregnant at 16* that almost glorify teen pregnancy, I wonder if our society has desensitized itself to the collective notion that teen pregnancy is no big deal, or worse—the new normal.

My mom was particularly worried that me or my sister would one day follow in our generational footsteps: my mother had my brother when she was 17, and my gramma had her at age 15. Although I never got pregnant in my teens, I was in disbelief for a long time when the reality set in that I was going to be a single parent.

July 21, 1990, 7:21 a.m.
I don't want to have a child. I don't want to give life to someone and bring them into this world. Then I have to try to make their life better for them than it was for me? Forget it!

In my journals growing up, I talked about not wanting children. I didn't want to bring anyone into this cruel, negative world. I liked kids in general, and I could deal with other people's kids because I could always give them back, but there were many aspects of childhood that I just didn't want to deal with on a daily basis. I knew I wouldn't be able to handle motherhood as a girl, and as of this writing, I still face challenges with it.

I became a single mother when my daughter was 10 months old. Single parenting was definitely not something I ever considered, and because of my struggle it's hard for me to fathom why women would either choose to raise children alone (with a sperm donor) or repeatedly have children out of wedlock. In this chapter I'll share my story as well as those of my friends who dealt with single motherhood as girls.

When I was a girl, if I heard that another girl was pregnant, it was a shocker. As I said earlier, sex certainly wasn't talked about much in church or Sunday School as I was growing up. I just knew it was wrong, it was taboo, and it wasn't discussed. In the seventh grade, I took a sex education class, and while I don't remember a lot about it, I doubt abstinence was a key part of the curriculum back then.

In high school, however, it was quite common to hear about girls having sex, getting pregnant, and having abortions. In 2010, the Guttmacher Institute reported that pregnancy and abortion rates increased in girls ages 15 to 19 for the first time in years. The increase may be attributed to the fact that in the years preceding the study, sex education classes focused only on abstinence, not on contraceptives. Don't think you're invincible, and you can't get pregnant the first time. It happens more often than you might think.

I felt like some people were in denial that it was happening, or just ignored it—especially adults. Then when the most "unlikely" people got pregnant out of wedlock, such as deacons' daughters, or a shy, quiet straight-A student, it seemed to be accepted, and sometimes, even admired. These were very confusing messages for me because I really didn't understand the issues that came with teen pregnancy and premarital sex.

TEEN MOMS

When I was 20, I helped two of my best friends deal with unplanned pregnancies, one right after the other.

The first time, it was Beth. Beth had been having sex the longest out of all of us in the group, and having not used condoms for years, she thought she couldn't get pregnant. Together, we went to a Planned Parenthood office one day because she was scared—she had missed her period and feared the worst. I sat in the waiting room the whole time she was with the doctor. When she came out, she didn't even look at me. Her face was red and she was crying, so I knew what was up. I was the first person to whom she uttered the words, "I'm pregnant."

When we got in the car, she put the key in the ignition but just sat there crying with the motor running. I switched places with her and drove her home, where we talked for a while. I can't imagine all the emotions she must have been feeling, and I'm glad I was there. The next day, she told me her parents and her boyfriend all encouraged her to get an abortion. But along with myself, Beth's other friends strongly disagreed with abortion. We let her know that we supported her regardless of her decision, and encouraged her to do what she felt was best—not anyone else.

On the morning of her abortion appointment, Beth decided that even though her life would become more difficult with another human being to care for and she wasn't quite ready to be a mom, she wasn't going to have the abortion after all. During the rest of her pregnancy, we continued to hang out, but not as much, since she was sometimes not feeling well or got sleepy earlier than usual. I never knew anyone else that close to me who was pregnant, so it was new to me. I didn't know about or understand all the changes that your body goes through during pregnancy, nor the fatigue that is common in the first trimester.

Her baby's father was emotionally abusive. He continued to treat her poorly, and although he was present for their son's birth, he didn't continue to be in Beth's life or their son's.

Beth named her son with the name I picked, and a few years later, she got married and had a daughter as well. I haven't seen Beth in several years, but I can say that motherhood changed Beth for the better. Her character improved, and she became unselfish. She really matured and stepped up to the challenge of motherhood at a young age. When the biological father of Beth's son tried to come back into their lives over a decade later, her son, regarding his stepfather as his father, did not choose to start a relationship with his biological father. I'm really happy for Beth and her family.

Another of my friends, Angela, worked alongside me at a part-time job for almost a year. While Beth was pregnant, Angela got pregnant as well. In Angela's case, she was intimate with a friend—one time—whom she wasn't actually dating or attracted to. At work one day, she was on the phone with her doctor who gave her the news. I was the only one in the room with her, so again I was the first to know. She got really quiet, and then cried. She was devastated, and we didn't get much work done that evening. Like Beth, she had her son without his father in his life, but she's managing fine without him. She didn't stop her life when she got pregnant. Since then, she's gotten married and has become a registered nurse. I'm proud of her.

Both Beth and Angela were fortunate to have encouraging friends when they needed them most. Anyone can hang around when times are good and people are having fun, but you don't know who your true friends are until you hit a rough patch like they did. With the help of their friends and families, both of these ladies stepped up to a remarkable challenge, but unfortunately, not everyone does.

The epidemic of broken homes and single parenthood cheats everyone. Some women intentionally choose to become single parents, but I can't give you that viewpoint because I never would have decided to become a parent on my own. Women who say you don't need a man to raise a child are technically correct, but if I could choose, I would have a good man with me.

Women can't give children everything they need emotionally and spiritually. As mothers, we can love them with all our being; we can buy them every book, toy, and gadget to help them become intelligent and develop skills; and we can put them in schools where they grow academically and socially, but we can't replace a man's influence. If you don't believe me, ask someone who never had a father or a father-figure in their life when they were growing up. Chances are, they'll tell you something was missing, and that they longed for that fatherly relationship. It has nothing to do with whether their mother's/aunt's/grandmother's methods of child-rearing were good enough.

**Even the most competent
single mothers cannot take the place
of a man's role and influence.**

THE UGLY TRUTH

The negative effects of growing up without a father have been scientifically documented. In its report, *Experiments in Living: The Fatherless Family by Civitas*, The Institute for the Study of Civil Society[4] found the following:

Lone mothers:
- Are poorer
- Are more likely to suffer from stress, depression, and other emotional and psychological problems
- Have more health problems
- May have more problems interacting with their children

Non-resident biological fathers:
- Are at risk of losing contact with their children
- Are more likely to have health problems and engage in high-risk behavior (drugs, unprotected sex, etc.)

Children living without their biological fathers:
- Are more likely to live in poverty and deprivation
- Have more trouble in school
- Tend to have more trouble getting along with others
- Have higher risk of health problems
- Are at greater risk of suffering physical, emotional, or sexual abuse
- Are more likely to run away from home

Teenagers living without their biological fathers are more likely to:
- Experience problems with sexual health
- Become teenage parents themselves
- Get into criminal activity
- Smoke, drink alcohol, and take drugs
- Skip school
- Be excluded from school
- Leave school at 16
- Have adjustment problems

Young adults who grew up not living with their biological fathers:
- Are less likely to attain qualifications
- Are more likely to experience unemployment
- Are more likely to have low income
- Are more likely be on public assistance (welfare)
- Are more likely to experience homelessness
- Are more likely to go to jail
- Are more likely to suffer from long-term emotional and psychological problems
- Are more likely to develop health problems
- Tend to enter marital relationships earlier but more often as a cohabitation arrangement

> ❧ Are more likely to divorce or dissolve their
> cohabiting unions
> ❧ Are more likely to have children outside marriage
> or outside any partnership

With all of the evidence, it's easy to see that single-parenting is not the way to go. Most people are not ready for it, and do not consider all of the effects (on themselves, their kids, and the people in their circle of influence).

MY BABY

I opened up to the idea of motherhood after I got married. I remember when my former husband Mike told me he was bored with his life as long as it was just he and I. He wanted to be a father more than anything, so I stopped getting the birth control shots that I had been on for years. I don't think I ever would have allowed myself to get pregnant if I knew I would end up being a single mother. I've always been independent and enjoyed my freedom. I love my daughter with all my heart, but I wish I had done things differently.

When Mike and I separated, we were moving from Maryland to Virginia. He decided to help me move everything but returned to Maryland temporarily before making his own move back to New York. My mother and sister knew we were having trouble, and they moved in with me to help out. I'll be forever grateful to my mother and sister for their support and help in raising my daughter, Kaia in those precious early years.

Even though I was in my late 20s, I felt completely inadequate as a mom. For the first year of my daughter's life, I looked at her as a beautiful baby that I didn't know what to do with. I doubted my capabilities as a mother because I didn't see myself as being a natural nurturer. I felt like I didn't know what I was doing, and I got impatient and frustrated with my daughter easily. She didn't sleep through the night with any regularity until well after age 2, and it was almost impossible to get her to nap.

This may sound silly or strange, but I found myself somewhat fearful of being alone with her when both my sister and my mother were out of the house. Kaia wasn't a "bad" child. She acted pretty normal for each developmental stage she was in, but ages 2 to 5 were really hard for me, dealing with potty training, tantrums, and not napping.

The next few years after that, I looked at my daughter as a responsibility and thought of her more in terms of how to get her to follow rules and be obedient than someone with whom I had a relationship. Kaia was a happy baby, and as a girl now, she still likes to smile, laugh, and hug people, whether she knows them or not. She will hug a server in a restaurant just as willingly as she would hug her favorite cousin.

Sometimes my anger and frustration escalated to the point where I was ready to put my hands on my daughter to try to discipline her. Hitting and spanking out of anger hurts you and your child, and it may not make them do the right thing next time—in fact, it might teach them to fear you—instead of teaching them to respect you. It made me feel guilty, and it made her more defiant, which means she was less compliant.

FROM BAD TO WORSE

In my case, my anger stemmed from frustration, impatience, lack of control, and helplessness. At times, my anger manifested as depression. I would dwell on why Kaia's father moved farther away from us instead of being closer to help me with her. He started another relationship during our separation, and I was resentful that his child from that relationship was seeing the financial and emotional benefits of having him around when Kaia didn't. Sometimes, I even thought about suicide, figuring irrationally that because I was such a failure as a person, Kaia would be better off without me, and I could be relieved from all the emotional pain of the separation and divorce.

Although I didn't miss living with Mike when we were separated, I still had to grieve about our relationship. I used to think self-defeating thoughts that no one else would want me because I had a baby, that I was stupid and deserved whatever treatment I got from Mike, or that no man would ever love me as much as he did. Sometimes I would drive over the bridges in town during my commute and think about jumping off. I reasoned that Kaia would be in good hands with my family, and that it wasn't a big loss if she never knew me (she was still a baby at the time).

SEEKING HELP

I had to get help to deal with all the negative emotions. As I said before, there's no shame in talking to a counselor or professional therapist who's trained in these matters.

I went to a community group and voluntarily took a couple of parenting classes that are sometimes court-ordered. I learned about ways to nurture my child. The classes gave me more self-confidence and hope, and I met my future best friend there as well.

God knew all this was going to happen, and in spite of all my mistakes, He has been taking care of me. I live well, have a very good job, and I'm able to provide needs and wants for myself and my daughter. He put people in my life to talk to and help me heal from the hurts of divorce. What started as a major setback became a setup—and God made it all possible. I could not have made it this far on my own.

BUT IF...

If you decide to have a child anyway at your young age, let me give you a bit more to think about.

No one asks to be born, so once you have kids, don't leave them hanging. They'll grow up knowing if they're unwanted or unloved. Do everything you can to support them and be the role model you may have never had.

I often hear people describe certain children as "bad." A person can excuse a child's behavior by shaking her head and saying, "She's bad." Sometimes we laugh it off, but when I think about it, it's really not funny to be referred to as "bad." What does this negative connotation do to a child's self-esteem? Are we calling kids "bad" because they don't behave? Do we not know more efficient, less-psychologically damaging methods of training our children than to spank them or call them "bad," even when those methods don't work to change their behavior for the better? Our society is so quick to label children, but it can cripple them. I caution you to be careful with your words because whatever you repeatedly tell a child about themselves, they'll come to believe.

Whatever you repeatedly tell a child about themselves, they will come to believe.

YOU DON'T HAVE TO BE SUPERWOMAN

Can you "have it all"? Maybe, but not necessarily all at once. Some people mistakenly assume that single people have more free time than others, but it's a whole new ball game when you're a single parent. Black women, especially those who are mothers, have a tendency to do things for everyone else and take care of themselves dead last. But sometimes you have to say no to people without feeling guilty about it. If you run yourself into the ground, how will all the things you need to do get done? Use self-care and get enough sleep—don't stay up too late watching TV, reading, talking on the phone, or using the internet. Don't sacrifice your peace. Treat yourself— take yourself to a movie, have ice cream, read a good book, or go to the spa. Don't answer the phone or do any chores. If you have kids, have a trusted friend, neighbor, or family member keep your kids overnight. Believe it or not, your kids need you to get some stress relief and energy—to deal with them!

And what if you don't yet have any children? If you have a mom, or someone in that role that takes care of you and looks out for you, think about how she may be feeling and be sensitive to that. Let's show some love and appreciation for our stressed, overworked, and caring mothers/mother-figures.

CONSIDER THIS

Where do you stand with parenthood? If you know you're not ready to be a mom, then don't have sex or talk about having children just to seem agreeable to a guy you like. If you're reading this and haven't yet had children, I encourage you to live your life as a single woman first. And if you don't want kids, that's OK (not all women should be mothers), but stick to your guns—don't let anyone talk you into it. There's so much to do, and children are a serious, life-long responsibility, not to be taken lightly. Once you conceive, they're on the way within nine months, whether you're ready or not.

Children are a serious, life-long responsibility, not to be taken lightly.

If you made a mistake, whether you had premarital sex and caught a disease, had a baby at a young age, had a miscarriage or abortion, you can recover. It's not too late. Start today. Try to understand why you made the decisions that got you into your situation. What were you thinking? What did you believe about yourself? About the guy you were dealing with? Does this behavior stem from abandonment issues or a negative or absent relationship with your father? As I keep stressing, there's absolutely no shame in talking to a therapist or other mental health professional about these issues. As Pastor Paula White of the show *Paula White Today* says, "You cannot conquer what you can't confront."

FURTHER READING
Are you having trouble coping with single motherhood? Release your stress and begin the healing process with Angela Thomas, who tells her personal story of raising four kids by herself with humor, candor and real-world insights in *My Single Mom Life: Stories and Practical Lessons for Your Journey.*

part four ~

THE WORLD IS YOURS

12

WHAT'S **WRONG** with work?

"Seek to do less and accomplish more, to achieve more. Doing is action. Achievement is successful action."[5]

— **A.J. RUSSELL** —

As early as age 13, I wondered why God put me here, but I didn't want to take the rest of my life to learn my purpose. I always did well in school, and I was taught that I had to do well in school so I could get a good job when I grew up. The question was, "What do I want to be when I grow up?" I was able to discover my purpose by paying attention to activities I felt drawn to, and gained satisfaction from.

Back in the day, many kids assumed that I liked school because I got good grades and knew the answers to questions in class. I had an aptitude to do well because I've always loved to read, and I did my homework. But at times I felt invisible, lonely, or unpopular outside the classroom.

What I didn't know then was that the social implications of being nerdy were nothing to fret about.

In this chapter, we'll discuss:

- ℘ The pressure of performance and approval
- ℘ How to discover your passion
- ℘ How to determine your purpose
- ℘ Researching your desired occupation

PERFORMANCE ANXIETY

Do you ever feel pressure to get good grades or feel anxious about working at your part-time job because of the scrutiny you receive? Or maybe a lot of people are counting on you to do well in a sporting event, or your parents are pushing you a little too hard to make a high grade on a test? Do you try to earn love, approval, or acceptance from the things you do for others?

My dad placed a high importance on education and getting good grades in school. He was the valedictorian of his high school class, and he took education very seriously, just like his dad did. One of the ways I could always get his approval was by making sure my report card had high marks.

Once at the admissions office of a college in Boston, my dad told the administrator that my grades were just OK, but he pointed at my little sister and said, "She's the straight-A student." I felt like he was undermining my good work by comparing us, and he wasn't comparing apples to apples. I got A's and B's (with a few C's here and there) throughout high school, but to him, it didn't seem to be good enough. I didn't know that years later, I would go on to become the first in the family to earn not one, but two college degrees before my siblings earned any. Earning top grades and degrees didn't make me better than they were or more worthy of success, but as a 17-year-old, my dad's statement had hurt my feelings and fostered a certain sense of competition and resentment.

We're human beings, not human doings. Your worth was established before you were conceived in your mother's womb, without you doing anything to earn it or deserve it. Your accomplishments may establish your value with some people, but don't let this be the reason why you excel. Take pride in yourself, and do so not to get noticed or to receive kudos but because you care how you represent yourself and God. This brings another song to mind:

> *"... but what you don't know is*
> *when she gets home and*
> *gets behind closed doors*
> *man, she hits the floor and*
> *what you can't see is*
> *she's on her knees*
> *so when you see her next time*
> *she'll tell ya*
> *'It's the God in me...'*
> *—Mary Mary, "God in Me"*

If you do receive compliments and kudos for your work, performance (music, sports or grades), or deeds, accept them humbly, referring back to God who gave you the talent and the strength to pull it all off. When people see that glorious glow—that sense of something special around you— He'll draw others to Him. And if no one seems to notice, don't despair—God sees it all.

We're human beings, not human doings.

WHAT DO YOU DO?

To compete for a satisfying career and have a comfortable lifestyle, you have to consider what you want your life to be like after you finish high school and how your education today will pay off tomorrow. Do you want to go to college or vocational school? Do you want to eventually run your own business or work for someone else? No one else can tell you what's right for you. For inspiration and ideas, check out *Black Enterprise* magazine, which often features some awesome profiles of kidpreneurs and teenpreneurs, and hosts the *Teenpreneurs Conference* every year.

One former teenpreneur of note is Ariana Pierce, an actress, motivational speaker and author who was one of *Black Enterprise's Entrepreneurs of the Week* in 2011. Pierce began speaking at national youth conferences at age 14, started her own business at age 17, and wrote four of her six books before age 20! As of this writing, she is the 21-year-old CEO of *Superstar Nail Lacquer*, a line of eco-friendly nail polish, which has been featured in national magazines and supported by celebrities. Pierce does it all while attending college full time at Michigan State University.

Media mogul Russell Simmons wrote a book entitled *Do You! 12 Laws to Access the Power In You to Achieve Happiness and Success*. In his book, he encourages people to walk in their "gifting"—that is, using their talents to achieve their goals and make a positive impact on their communities. In other words, what are you so passionate about that you would do it for free, with or without recognition? Do you have any hobbies that you could turn into a business? Do you get compliments for something you enjoy, that takes little effort for you because it just seems to come naturally? What are you really good at? Who could be helped or served with your talents? Whatever your ideas are, choose something that:

a) you enjoy,

b) uses your God-given talents, and

c) will pay the bills.

Until you get to "c," it's just a hobby—but that doesn't mean you shouldn't keep at it and perfect your craft until you can make a living out of it.

The problem with many adults in the workforce is they're unhappy because they focus more on "c" than anything else. Who wants to get up every morning to rush into traffic so they can spend 8 to 10 hours in a place they hate? But lots of people do it because they feel stuck without many options or have no ambition to change jobs or careers. You don't have that problem because you're young and you can start today on the right path.

What if you have a lot of interests and are good at doing more than one thing—how do you narrow it down? I'm like that. I have so many thoughts and ideas that I often float from one project to another without fully completing each one before it. But the answer is you don't have to choose. As a multi-faceted person, I have more than one business card, more than one website, and many aspects that make up who I am. You just have to focus on one major goal at a time. It's about quality, not quantity. You'll put in the time and produce a quality product if you're passionate about it.

A SENSE OF DIRECTION

If you ever need to find your way through a mall, you can go to a directory and look at the map. A yellow sticker is placed on the map that reads, "YOU ARE HERE." That's your reference point. From there, you can figure out how to get where you want to go.

Do you know where you are, and where you're headed? Do you know where you want to be? Do you have any goals for this year or the next?

The answers to these questions lie in discovering and learning God's purpose for you. You find your purpose by listening to that voice within. Once you tune in, you'll find signs along the way that point to where your talents are. As Bishop George Bloomer of Bethel Family Worship Center explains it, "If you want to know what God's purpose is in your life, you've got to please Him, and in pleasing God, your purpose is revealed to you. Your purpose may be covered in a number of assignments. I worked in various areas of ministry until I stumbled upon the thing that felt right. God spoke to me through a growing awareness, through open doors, through closed doors, and through heavy impressions on my heart."

If you really don't know where to start, pray for wisdom and insight. Take a career interest inventory such as the Myers-Briggs Type Indicator (which you can find online or through your guidance counselor or career office at school) or a ministry gifts survey (often distributed in member-ship/discipleship classes when you join a church). Read some good career/ vocational books, such as *What Color Is Your Parachute?* Volunteering is a great way to get involved while you test the waters. Churches, schools (tutoring), shelters, hospitals, nursing homes, political campaigns, walks/races for foundations, and other nonprofit groups could all use your help!

Everyone is good at something. Ask yourself:

- ☞ What can I focus on besides being popular, fitting in, or getting a certain guy to like me?
- ☞ What am I good at?
- ☞ What do I like to do?

◦ What makes me feel good?
◦ What kind of work would I do for free?

Your answers may not be popular with your friends, but remember, that's OK. It's OK to be different. Be who God made you to be. Do you.

WRITE THE VISION
Once you have your goal and know where you want to be, the next step is to visualize it and what it would feel like to achieve it. Do your research to find out what it takes to get where you want to be, then list the baby steps to get there. Your steps should be measurable, quantifiable and written.

**You can work hard,
or you can work smart.
Use a strategy to succeed.**

To help you formulate a solid plan for success, I recommend you read a good business book, such as *Climbing the Ladder in Stilettos: 10 Strategies for Stepping Up to Success at Work* by Lynette Lewis. In her book, Lewis gives tips on how to create a purpose statement and action plan to craft a career and life plan, not just a job. As she explains it, a purpose statement contains a verb (what you will do) and a condition or problem that exists, which you will change, and how it will affect others. For example, a purpose statement could be, "My purpose is to decrease the instances of HIV and AIDS in my community by visiting schools and educating people about myths and giving them tools to protect themselves."

In addition, Lewis emphasizes the advantage of creating a personal "board of directors" or a mastermind group that can serve to mentor you or advise you as you progress through your steps. This mastermind group is like having a team of mentors who can advise you, and whom you can bounce ideas off of when you're unsure of an important career decision you want to make.

Now that you've planned the work, it's time to work the plan.

WORKING SMART

You can work hard, or you can work smart. Working hard means you're putting a lot of time and energy into something without doing all your research, counting the costs, and making sure you're investing your time wisely. Working smart means that what you're doing now will result in dividends later (and I don't just mean financial gain). Working smart means you're using a strategy to succeed.

The single most important thing you can do to help yourself in high school, college, and beyond, is to keep reading and doing your homework (your research). It will always pay off for you, no matter how old you are, or what kind of career you pursue. Feeding your brain by reading the right kinds of books and publications will sharpen your mind, build your vocabulary, broaden your imagination, and challenge you to set and achieve goals.

> **Reading will sharpen your mind, broaden your imagination, and challenge you to set and achieve goals.**

... Reward is a brainwashed kid goin' wild
Young little girls already have a child
(Bad company) and now ya been framed
(The parents are hurtin') hurtin' and ashamed
(You're ruining yourself) and your mommy can't cope
Hey little kids don't follow these dopes
(As a rule from a non-fool) your life don't drool
Don't be a fool like those that don't go to school
(Get ahead) and accomplish things
You'll see the wonder and the joy life brings
(Don't admire thieves) hey, they don't admire you
Their times limited, hard rocks too
So listen be strong, scream 'whoopee doo'
Go for yours 'cause dreams come true...
—Slick Rick, "Hey Young World"

TAKE A CLOSER LOOK

Once you've done your due diligence (taken a career interest inventory and answered the questions in "A Sense of Direction"), it's time to use your research and find someone in your network to contact who's working in your desired field. Request an informational interview to get a feel for what their career entails, asking them questions such as:

- ☞ What do you like about this career?
- ☞ What do you dislike about this career?
- ☞ What kind of education, skills, and personality should I have if I want to pursue this type of career?
- ☞ Where can I find a part-time position, apprenticeship or internship to get some hands-on training and experience?

After the interview, you still have more work to do:

1. Write a thank-you note to the person, thanking them for their time and information. Send the note as soon as possible after the interview.

2. Decide whether you want to continue to research and pursue this career.

3. If you are still interested in this career, create an action plan to move further, using the resources cited. If not, research another one of interest and conduct a new informational interview.

CONSIDER THIS

Some people say life is too short to get up every day and go to work doing something they don't love. I'll say this: Life feels long if you make the wrong choices and get "stuck" along the way.

Life feels long if you make the wrong choices and get "stuck" in a miserable lifestyle.

You have time while you're in school to start thinking about your future plans, but don't worry if you're undecided or unsure. The questions you have are natural, but trusting in God to have control allows you to stop worrying and let Him handle it. As the Creator and ultimate planner of our lives, He knows what's best for you. If you follow His will, you'll be able to sit back and watch in amazement as life unfolds. Believe me, if you had asked me 10 years ago, I would have never guessed that my life would have progressed to where I am now, with my personal and professional accomplishments.

Depending on your environment and the job or career you're interested in, you may not have as much financial or emotional support to pursue it as you need. That's why it's a good idea to be cautious and choosy about whom you confide in. You can always apply for grants or scholarships—where there's a will, there's a way. God doesn't put dreams in our hearts just to make them ache. We must act to see those dreams come to fruition. Disassociate from people who try to crush your excitement, kill your dream, or discourage you from your goal.

At times you may feel overwhelmed under the pressure of perfection or someone else's approval—or maybe even feel like you're pushing yourself too hard—but don't give up. Stay the course with determination and focus. Study your craft, stay under the authority of your mentors and supervisors at work (especially if they have valuable experience and wisdom you can learn from). Keep the right attitude and be open-minded. Have integrity and do what's right versus what's easy. Be proud of your accomplishments and celebrate even the little successes along the way. Anything worth having is worth working for, and nothing worthwhile comes easy!

Hey young girl—the world is yours.

FURTHER READING

Some say that "job" stands for "just over broke." So don't get a job. If you're ready to get focused on the next steps after high school, don't sit around bored or restless. Do some research with Carol Christen and Richard Nelson Bolles' *What Color Is Your Parachute? For Teens, 2nd Edition: Discovering Yourself, Defining Your Future* and Russell Simmons' *Do You! 12 Laws to Access the Power in You to Achieve Happiness and Success*. If you've finished high school, you'll be well served by Lynette Lewis' *Climbing the Ladder in Stilettos: 10 Strategies for Stepping Up to Success at Work* as an indispensable guide to your working life.

13

WHAT'S **WRONG** with my money?

"People first, then money, then things."
— SUZE ORMAN —

*H*ave you ever looked at something days or weeks after you bought it, and wondered why you ever bought it? Do you go in your closet and notice items with the tags still on them? If so, this chapter is for you.

Or maybe you've received your first credit card (either just yours or co-signed with your parents), and you like to hit the mall every weekend just for the heck of it. Then this chapter is for you, too.

I can't give you much advice on investing, but I can advise you on philosophies that will keep you out of financial ruin and help you avoid "stupid tax," a term coined by financial expert Dave Ramsey. Saving money, paying for things with cash/debit cards, and avoiding credit cards will help you reach your financial goals and keep you out of the poorhouse.

SAVING MONEY

One thing I loved as a girl was music. I couldn't get enough of R&B and hip-hop. I had a small collection of vinyl records—the ones disc jockeys/deejays (DJs) now use at parties—and mix tapes. You can download music and remixed songs anytime from the internet, but in my day, if you wanted a remix, blend, or other special version of a song, you either had to find it on a CD single, cassette single, or get the 12-inch vinyl record from a DJ or a store that DJs went to. I remember getting $10 for every good report card and saving the money in my jewelry box so I could buy a cassette tape with it (those came before CDs). This was my earliest memory of saving money.

However, a traditional savings account or a different type of CD (a certificate of deposit) is a better savings instrument than a jewelry box. This also ensures that your big brother can't help himself to it like mine did! Having these funds in a bank or credit union gives you some security, as the accounts pay interest (CDs more so than savings accounts), and the funds are relatively easy to withdraw for emergencies. They may even have special accounts just for students or certain savings goals (Christmas or vacation accounts, for example).

Set aside a certain amount every paycheck that gets automatically direct-deposited into a savings account or money market fund that you don't touch unless it's for an emergency or other long-term saving goal. (Your employer can set up the direct deposit for you so you don't miss the money.) If you spend everything you make when you get your paycheck, and you never save for emergencies, you risk finding yourself in a tough spot.

The key to financial freedom is not necessarily making more money; it's spending less than you have and growing the amount you keep. When you decide to save $10, $20, $50, or

$100 consistently out of every paycheck, your wealth will grow. As Americans, we often overextend our spending budget by using credit cards in an undisciplined, careless fashion.

CREDIT—DON'T GET IT!

Mo' money, mo' problems? How about no money, mo' problems? Debt is no joke. Do you know how much trouble you can get into by mismanaging a credit card? If you're not responsible, you could cause a lifetime of debt woes and economic instability just by making a few careless charges, or even co-signing a loan for someone who falls on hard times or splits, leaving you with the bill.

In America, we treat credit like a necessity. People start businesses on credit, buy houses and cars with loans, and don't find it feasible to wait until they have enough cash or capital to begin spending. Who wants to wait?

When I started college, it was nothing for credit card companies to target students with offers. They lured you with free stuff—all you had to do was fill out a simple application, and even if you didn't have a job, you could get a credit card. At the time, I worked at Burger King on campus, and I made something like $5 an hour, but I was able to get a card with $500 on it. That amount doesn't sound like much, but at 17, if you owe it and you have no money—it's a lot!

Credit card companies market to us hard, selling the myth that you can own things today by promising tomorrow's income—which is never truly promised. You sacrifice your future peace for today's simple pleasures, and depending on how big of a hole you dig and the interest the credit card companies pile on over time, it feels like you'll never catch up. Many businesses use your credit score to determine what insurance and loan rates to offer you, whether they'll lend to you, let you lease an apartment, or offer you a job.

Credit card companies sell the myth that you can own things today by promising tomorrow's income—which is not promised.

Marketing messages browbeat us everywhere in the media, whether it's TV, radio, magazine ads, billboards on highways, and even TVs while we're in stores. They hype us up to think that the next big thing is more fashionable or better than the last because of the celebrity endorsing it, or that XYZ will solve our problems with such-and-such. Often, we make impulse purchases just because an item is nearby—not because we planned on buying it out of want or need. Like children, we don't consider buying something until we see it. But once we see it, we want it. And so we see, we want, and we spend. Left unchecked, it becomes a vicious cycle.

At the stage of life you're in, you don't need a credit card. The majority of pundits out there would disagree with me, but whatever you would do with a credit card, you can do with a debit card, interest free. If you feel you must have one, leave it at just one, with a relatively low limit of $1,000 or less (depending on your income and what you can realistically pay back at the end of the month without carrying a balance).

I strongly urge you not to open store cards (those offered by your favorite department or clothing stores), even though they run so-called sales and have discounts for cardholders. They have the highest interest rates. What's the logic of saving 10 percent today but paying through the nose when they inundate your email inbox with sales so that you'll charge more than you can pay off that month at ridiculous interest rates? Take this example, assuming the use of a store card at 28 percent interest:

Shoes: $98 on May 4 minus 10 percent new account discount = $88.20

Statement #1: Minimum payment of $10 due by June 15. You pay it and your new balance = $78.20.

Statement #2: Your balance from last month of $78.20 x 0.0183 (28 percent interest) + $78.20 = $79.43. They calculate a new minimum payment (not to mention whatever else you charged during the month).

When you don't pay your entire balance due each month, your balance continues to increase because the lender adds interest charges to each statement. Thus, you end up paying more for the item than you initially thought.

Get your discount up front by paying with cash or a debit card—you won't get a bill for it next month! You'll never regret it, and you'll probably spend less, because when you have to pay cash, you see the bills leaving your hand and you have to really think about it. Swiping a card in a machine doesn't have the same psychological effect. Having a lighter wallet or purse does. (And as long as you keep your receipt, you can get a refund or store credit most of the time.) Your savings will come from paying in cash and using a budget for non-essential items.

THE B-WORD

Yes, I said the dreaded b-word. But budgets are our friends. Author, speaker, and former pastor John C. Maxwell says that a budget tells your money what to do, instead of you trying to figure out where it went. Simply put, when you create a budget, you fill out a list of expenses you have, how much you pay toward them from each check, and see what your total is. A sample system for budgeting could be to divide your paycheck into categories, such as allocating 10 percent of your pay to charity or church, 10 percent to savings, and the remaining 80 percent divided among other budgeting categories (clothes, school supplies, transportation, trips, and so on).

If you find that your expenses exceed your income, you need to cut back on some things. This is usually where people in financial trouble whip out their credit card to make up for the shortfall, and it becomes a crutch until it's maxed out. This method also digs a financial grave of debt that is extremely difficult to climb out of because of compound interest, and you'll find that the companies that once tried to target you aggressively, offering their credit cards to you left and right, suddenly won't lend to you anymore.

Some places will tell you that you need good credit to rent an apartment or a car, but if you have cash and proof of employment, you can get around it. Avoiding debt is the best way to go.

Bottom line: If you don't have the cash right now to buy something, you probably can't afford it. Leave it alone, and if you really need it, go back and get it when you've got the money and the item is in line with your priorities. (It kills me when I hear that someone is getting their nails done, detailing their car, etc., but their rent is consistently late. Something is off, and it's probably the lights!)

If you don't have the cash right now to buy something, you probably can't afford it.

GIVING BACK

Giving money to charity is never a waste (barring a scam)—it always comes back to you. Tithing (the biblical principle of giving 10 percent of your income) is not about denial, it's about discipline, faith and stewardship. Those of us who tithe believe that we're just giving a portion of what God has already given to us. And as one of my pastors says, if you're faithful to tithe 10 percent, God will bless the 90 percent you have left. A tight fist cannot receive anything more, but an open hand can.

Different financial experts use different calculations for determining how to divide your income for savings, charitable giving, housing expenditures, etc., but I'll tell you one thing I know for sure: If you don't purposely set aside a percentage of your money in your budget for charity and savings, you will spend it.

Even if you don't believe in tithing or have a steady income to donate each month, you can still give back by volunteering. Share your knowledge, time, and talent with someone (I'll address this more in Chapter 12, "What's Wrong With Work?").

CONSIDER THIS

It's fun to buy stuff. It's OK to like nice things. But if you're the person at the beginning of this chapter who has lots of new, unused, unworn items in your closet, you need to ask yourself why you're spending. Is it to be social? Are you bored, unhappy, or feeling insecure? Are you trying to get over a breakup or look like someone you admire? Are you grieving a loss or feeling lonely? Are you trying to impress someone who doesn't like you as you are?

Spending money you don't have makes as much sense as overeating or undereating because it's self-destructive behavior. Recognize why you're spending money and consider whether you're using money or credit as a coping mechanism for a negative emotion or situation you haven't dealt with.

FURTHER READING

If you have a part-time job, get your financial plan together with *The Money Book for the Young, Fabulous, and Broke* by Suze Orman and Dave Ramsey's book *The Total Money Makeover*, which includes his "7 Baby Steps" and budgeting worksheets.

14

WHAT'S **WRONG** with church?

"Don't run to the phone, run to the throne."

— JOYCE MEYER —

hurch has been an integral part of the Black community for decades. From the old Negro spirituals that originated in slavery to the Civil Rights movement in the '60s, church has always been there.

In this chapter, I will discuss:

- spiritual beliefs,
- holding on to your faith,
- having quiet time with God,
- building your relationship with God, and
- the importance of fellowship with others who share your beliefs.

WHAT DO YOU BELIEVE?

What shapes your beliefs? Is it what you're taught at home or in church? What your friends say? What some guy you liked told you? Something that you're experiencing right now that seems to be doing no good?

I was raised in church. I don't remember ever not going to church or having the choice. I participated in countless skits, plays, and pageants, and I was always in Sunday School and morning worship. I may have had questions about my beliefs, but I didn't question my beliefs. In elementary school, several children were dismissed on Wednesdays at 2:30 p.m. for "religion," as they called it—a service for Catholics in our class. Everyone in my class, except for about eight of us attended. But no one ever mentioned God in school because you weren't supposed to, and the foul language I heard every day at school from the other kids was anything but religious.

I remember the first time someone challenged my beliefs. In the fifth grade a girl told me that the creation story (Adam and Eve) was a myth. (She was one of the kids who went to religion, too.) I don't remember the whole argument, but I dismissed her theory because my faith in God and the Bible was strong—I wasn't going to be swayed from what I believed.

In high school, I met many people with diverse backgrounds and beliefs about God, life, and the universe, including atheists (people who do not believe God exists) and agnostics (people who are not sure whether God exists). Oddly enough, my first boyfriend Steve was an atheist. Looking back, I didn't have a good reason to be with him. But at the time, I just wanted to be with whomever I wanted, without a thought about what was pleasing to God, or living life by His standards. It's no wonder I had all the issues and heartache that I did. We didn't have the same values, so our relationship was doomed from the start.

Sometimes people will let you down, even at church. Especially at church. Many wounded people are in the church—hurt by Christians, who are supposed to be there to love and help each person who comes through its doors.

Various situations will cause a person to completely discount religion, Christianity, and the church. I know plenty of people who stopped going to church—not because of the message being taught in the church, but because of the people inside the church who didn't seem to be living that message. My sister stopped going to church for a while when some of the church leaders began to mistreat my mother, suspecting her of adultery with our new pastor.

KEEP THE FAITH

At the church where I grew up, we had the same pastor for many years until he died. It took a long time for the church to find a new pastor, but when they did, that new pastor became good friends with my mother. By this time, I was a teenager, and he used to visit our house on many occasions, including one with his wife and one of his daughters who was the same age as my little sister.

A lot of gossip went around my church because of my mother's friendship with the pastor. I heard the rumors started with his wife, referred to as the "first lady." I don't know why, but she was very insecure and jealous of my mother and did many things to try to undermine her, including calling my father at work to tell him about their alleged affair, and turning deacons, Sunday School teachers and others against my mother, trying to assassinate her character.

The first lady sometimes came to my mother's job and harassed her. People didn't believe the first lady was crazy until they saw it for themselves one day, when she threatened my mother during a full Sunday School class where my mother taught preschoolers! The first lady even turned her youngest daughter away from us, and she stopped being friends with my sister.

One day when the pastor was leaving my house, he addressed the situation with my sister and I, directly. The conversation went something like this:

"Girls, I want to tell you something. Don't lose faith because of what has been going on and what people are saying about me and your mother. I know you girls are very close to your mom and this is bothering you, but don't lose faith in God."

"We haven't, Pastor," I said, as my sister looked on.

"This situation will make us all stronger," he said. "Your mom is a dear friend of mine. I look at you all as my extended family, and I love you."

"I get all of that, Pastor, but then how come you parked two blocks away from our house?" I asked, thinking someone might notice and start more gossip.

"People love to gossip—it's a fact of life," he explained.

"Your daughter didn't speak to me last night at church, and she doesn't speak to my sister at school," I said.

"She probably would have," he said, "but this situation is affecting her as well as you two."

Not long after that, a church meeting was held to decide whether to fire the pastor. Any member was allowed to have a say. My sister, about 12 at the time, spoke her peace in front of the congregation and walked out, as my mother sat quietly, crocheting something. My sister was very hurt by the sentiments about my mother having an affair with the pastor, but my mother didn't try to defend herself. Eventually the board decided to vote the pastor out of office. My mother continued teaching Sunday School, and most of the people who turned against her apologized.

The pastor moved back to his hometown of New York City, and he got divorced but stayed in touch with my mother for some time. Sadly, after he lost touch with my mother, she got an email from a mutual friend saying that he had died from cancer—about 10 years after his conversation with us.

RELIGION OR RELATIONSHIP?

I don't know how many of the people who spoke against my mother had a close relationship with God, but she had to rely on hers to get through the ordeal. This was a church my mother had been a faithful member of, Sunday School teacher, and active participant in the ministry for more than a decade. Everyone knew her—yet she was still judged unfairly and talked about.

Yes, sometimes bad things happen to good people. There are many reasons why God allows us to go through trials and hard times, whether it was our fault or not. As one of my pastors says, "A storm with Jesus is a whole lot better than a storm without Jesus."

I used to think I knew God because I was raised in church. Even after my baptism, I believed in Him as Lord, but I didn't allow Him to be Lord over my life. I prayed to God when I had a problem or a request, but I didn't talk much to Him any other time. I had to go through a lot in my marriage and divorce before I really started to pray regularly and learn to trust God in the good times, not just ask Him for help in the bad times.

Religion does not equal relationship. Going to church every week and participating in different ministry activities isn't a relationship. Talking with God and reading His Word (the Bible), and involving Him in your life decisions is.

Having a relationship with Him allows you to see yourself the way He sees you, and love yourself as He loves you—

unconditionally. His love isn't based on what you do but because of who you are—His child! With that kind of love and reassurance, you don't need to seek attention or affection from a guy. A guy worthy of you will notice your God-like characteristics and be drawn to you for the right reasons, such as your personality, your values, your intelligence and your achievements.

CONVERSATIONS WITH GOD

Don't believe everything you hear—not even what I'm writing here with my scriptural references (check the back of the book—I've got 'em)! Do your own research. Even when you hear something from the pulpit, from a person you respect, go back to the Bible and read it for yourself, no matter how truthful (or unbelievable) it sounds. I can assure you, if you pray and ask God to reveal Himself, His Word will speak to you and your situation. Once you know that you know something for yourself, no one can take it away from you or sway your faith.

Get in the habit of talking to Him throughout the day—wherever you are. It doesn't have to be a formal occasion. You can talk to God like you'd talk to one of your girlfriends. Coming to Him in reverence is not the same as coming to Him with formality. You can be real with Him—big words and the King James-style Elizabethan Bible language aren't required.

You don't need to go through anyone to get to God. He's available to you anywhere, anytime.

You don't have to go to a priest to reach God. He's always there, ready to listen and offer guidance. When Jesus died on the cross for our sins more than 2,000 years ago, He went to God on our behalf, and since then, you don't need an intermediary to get to God. You don't have to wait until you get to church or get in your closet on your knees for Him to hear you.

Some may feel it's wrong to pray for things that aren't "spiritual," but God wants to talk to us about everything that goes on in our lives, big or small. As author Joyce Meyer says, "To God, everything is small stuff." Nothing is too insignificant for us to discuss or too big, crazy, or out of control for Him to handle. He's the ruler of the universe, and He wants to be your BFF. Regular conversations about your day, your joys, and your struggles—let Him have it! He can take it. You don't have to hold back. Yes, He knows it all anyway, but you still need to get it out. You can go to Him with anything and trust that He will take care of you. Now who else can you say that about?

**To God, everything is small stuff.
No matter what's on your mind,
He can handle it.**

CONSIDER THIS

No matter where I've lived, I've always been a member of a predominantly Black church. I'm sure other churches of different denominations and racial makeups have similar issues to the ones I've encountered. People are people, no matter where they are. There's no perfect church in this world, because there are no perfect people. Just because someone in the ministry or on church staff hurts your feelings or betrays you, it's not enough reason to change churches or abandon them altogether.

In the Bible, Hebrews 10:25 encourages us to fellowship with other believers to encourage each other and reinforce our faith. I can tell a big difference in my attitude and my psyche if I miss more than three consecutive weeks of church at a time. That's why it's so important for us to not become isolated, spend time with friends who share the same values we do, and not lose connections with other believers.

If someone betrays you, ask God for guidance and keep going. A great example of this is the story of David and King Saul in the Bible (1 and 2 Samuel). The church's programs, ministries, teaching, and activities should help you grow in your relationship with Jesus, complementing your own quiet time with God (you don't expect to get everything from a sermon once a week, do you?), If not, then that's a clearer sign for you to exit, but don't forget to consult God first. Bottom line—if God calls you to a church, do not move until He releases you from it.

> **If God calls you to a church, do not move until He releases you from it.**

To some people, there's no difference between Christians, others who go to church, and the rest of the world. Christians are no better or more perfect than anyone else, but we strive to live right because we believe in Jesus Christ. We're supposed to stand out as the light of the world, always striving to be like Jesus, in spite of our human nature and sinfulness working against us. How would you feel if someone only called you when they needed something from you? Would you wonder if they care about what's going on with you? Then why do we treat God that way?

We always need to be prepared to explain what we believe and why (see 1 Peter 3:15-16). Certain people will come around to challenge you, whether they're atheist, agnostic, or just annoying. But if you're firm in your faith, no one can sway you or cause you to doubt what you believe. If you have questions about your church or religious beliefs, ask someone knowledgeable who you trust, like a Sunday School teacher or a minister. They've studied the Bible for years and may even have taken classes to gain knowledge that can help you answer some of the hard questions you may have. And, of course, pray for continued insight and discernment.

FURTHER READING

Are you jaded by church? Are you unsure whom or what to believe? Kirk Franklin's *The Blueprint: A Plan for Living Above Life's Storms* and Nancy Leigh DeMoss and Dannah Gresh's exposé *Lies Young Women Believe: And the Truth that Sets Them Free* will challenge your beliefs and give you some down-to-earth perspective on heavenly and worldly things.

15

WHAT'S **WRONG** with you? Nothing!!

> "Goals and dreams are one and the same.
> Just say you believe and both you will attain."
>
> — **HILL HARPER** —

For years, I put myself down, asking myself, "What's wrong with me?" But I eventually realized that I had to ask, "What's right with me?" So here we are, at the end of this book, which hopefully answers the question of what's wrong with you: Nothing!

You may still have many concerns about what is going on in your life, why you look the way you do, feel the way you do, talk the way you do, relate to others they way you do, and believe in the things you were taught. And the journey is not over.

The journey to finding yourself and accepting yourself as you are does not end when you finish reading this chapter. It doesn't even end when you become an adult. It's a life-long process. For whatever area, whatever circumstance that you think that life has failed you, or that you have failed yourself, please—do not give up. It gets better.

My favorite chapter of Scripture is Philippians 4, which is part of a hopeful letter that Jesus' apostle Paul, wrote to the ancient church in Philippi from jail:

> *"I am not saying this because I am in need, for I have learned to be content whatever the circumstances. I know what it is to be in need, and I know what it is to have plenty. I have learned the secret of being content in any and every situation, whether well fed or hungry, whether living in plenty or in want. I can do everything through him who gives me strength."*
> **(Philippians 4:11-13 NIV)**

If Paul could be content in prison with all he had to endure, what does that say about your situation? Even if it seems like you're in mental prison, you don't have to stay there. No matter what problems you have to deal with, you can rely on Jesus Christ to be your strength.

YOU NEED HIM

If your circumstances have caused you to lose your way, doubt God, or feel like giving up, then maybe you need to start fresh. Give yourself another chance. Whether you need to reacquaint yourself with God, accept Jesus as your personal Savior, go back to a church you left, or find a new church—whatever it is, it's not too late to get started back on the right path.

If you haven't accepted Jesus Christ as your personal Savior, you can do it right now. You can say a simple prayer like this one:

Lord, I need you. I am a sinner and I can't make it in this life without you. I ask you to come into my heart, lead me and guide me. Be my best friend. Give me the strength and wisdom to live for you for the rest of my life.

And that's it—you're saved! As Paul writes: "If you confess with your mouth 'Jesus is Lord' and believe in your heart that God raised him from the dead, you will be saved. For it is with your heart that you believe and are justified, and it is with your mouth that you confess and are saved." (Romans 10:9-10 NIV)

From here, I recommend that you find a Bible-based church where you can learn the principles of discipleship to grow in your Christian walk, and get baptized if you have never been. Being baptized as Jesus was is an outward symbol to the world that you have become saved and born again, but the prayer of salvation (the prayer where you confess your sin) along with your belief is what saves you—not the water you're briefly submerged in.

YOU ARE DESTINED FOR GREATNESS!

It's high time you decide what you want. What greatness can you accomplish? Prepare, and make yourself mentally available for the opportunity. Invest in yourself, and set goals. Where do you want to be this time next year? In five years? How do you want your life to be different from the way it is today? What would you want to change? What is in your control? What do you need to make peace with?

Financial guru Suze Orman says, "You've got to face it to erase it." If you face your fears, you can overcome your insecurities and move forward. Everything you need is with you and around you, and if you don't see it yet, don't worry, it's coming. God hasn't brought you this far to leave you.

Where you started out in life doesn't determine where or how you'll end up. Your past can affect your future, but it doesn't have to solidify your fate. However, you do reap what you sow. Self-control in the areas of eating, money, and sex can go a long way to keep you on the path to success.

It's up to you to decide who you'll become. You can walk the wide, easy path of mediocrity and compromise that the world takes, which leads to destruction, or the narrow, more challenging path designed specifically for you by your Creator. You will be well-rewarded for your effort.

> *"I do not consider myself yet to have taken hold of it. But one thing I do: Forgetting what is behind and straining toward what is ahead, I press on toward the goal to win the prize for which God has called me heavenward in Christ Jesus."*
> **(Philippians 3:13-14 NIV)**

FURTHER READING

Did you enjoy this book? Hill Harper's *Letters to a Young Sister: DeF.I.N.E. Your Destiny* and *The Real Deal: A Spiritual Guide for Black Teen Girls* by Billie Montgomery Cook are similar books like it that inspired me, and will inspire you, too. So enjoy, and keep shining like the star you are!

references

SCRIPTURE REFERENCES

All of the scripture references listed below were mentioned earlier in the book and are provided here for easy reference. All these verses are listed from different translations of the Bible as noted:

- ❧ The Amplified Bible (AMP)
- ❧ Contemporary English Version (CEV)
- ❧ The Message (MSG)
- ❧ New International Version (NIV)
- ❧ New King James Version (NKJV)
- ❧ New Living Translation (NLT)

DEDICATION

"All praise to God, the Father of our Lord Jesus Christ. God is our merciful Father and the source of all comfort. He comforts us in all our troubles so that we can comfort others. When they are troubled, we will be able to give them the same comfort God has given us."
(1 Corinthians 1:3-4 NIV)

INTRODUCTION

"It's in Christ that we find out who we are and what we are living for. Long before we first heard of Christ and got our hopes up, he had his eye on us, had designs on us for glorious living, part of the overall purpose he is working out in everything and everyone."
(Ephesians 1:11-12 MSG)

2

"Thank you for making me so wonderfully complex! Your workmanship is marvelous — how well I know it."
(Psalm 139:14 NLT)

3

"The second most important commandment says: 'Love others as much as you love yourself.' No other commandment is more important than these."
(Mark 12:31 CEV)

"I can do all things through Christ who strengthens me."
(Philippians 4:13 NKJV)

6

"But the LORD said to Samuel, 'Do not consider his appearance or his height, for I have rejected him. The LORD does not look at the things human beings look at. People look at the outward appearance, but the LORD looks at the heart.'"
(1 Samuel 16:7 NIV)

"For I know the plans I have for you," declares the LORD, "plans to prosper you and not to harm you, plans to give you hope and a future."
(Jeremiah 29:11 NIV)

7

*"Do you not know that the wicked will not inherit
the kingdom of God? Do not be deceived: Neither
the sexually immoral nor idolaters nor adulterers nor
male prostitutes nor homosexual offenders nor
thieves nor the greedy nor drunkards nor slanderers
nor swindlers will inherit the kingdom of God."*
(1 Corinthians 6:9-10 NIV)

10

*"So each husband should love his wife as much as he loves
himself, and each wife should respect her husband."*
(Ephesians 5:33 CEV)

*"The heart is hopelessly dark and deceitful, a puzzle
that no one can figure out. But I, God, search the
heart and examine the mind. I get to the heart of the
human. I get to the root of things. I treat them as
they really are, not as they pretend to be."*
(Jeremiah 17:9-10 *The Message***)**

14

*"Some people have gotten out of the habit of meeting
for worship, but we must not do that. We should keep on
encouraging each other, especially since you know that
the day of the Lord's coming is getting* closer."
(Hebrews 10:25 CEV)

*"Instead, you must worship Christ as Lord of your life.
And if someone asks about your Christian hope, always be
ready to explain it. But do this in a gentle and respectful
way. Keep your conscience clear. Then if people speak
against you, they will be ashamed when they see what
a good life you live because you belong to Christ."*
(1 Peter 3:15-16 NLT)

15

"I am not saying this because I am in need, for I have learned to be content whatever the circumstances. I know what it is to be in need, and I know what it is to have plenty. I have learned the secret of being content in any and every situation, whether well fed or hungry, whether living in plenty or in want. I can do everything through him who gives me strength."
(Philippians 4:11-13 NIV)

"Enter through the narrow gate. For wide is the gate and broad is the road that leads to destruction, and many enter through it. But small is the gate and narrow the road that leads to life, and only a few find it."
(Matthew 7:13-14 NIV)

"If you confess with your mouth 'Jesus is Lord' and believe in your heart that God raised him from the dead, you will be saved. For it is with your heart that you believe and are justified, and it is with your mouth that you confess and are saved."
(Romans 10:9-10 NIV).

"I do not consider myself yet to have taken hold of it. But one thing I do: Forgetting what is behind and straining toward what is ahead, I press on toward the goal to win the prize for which God has called me heavenward in Christ Jesus."
(Philippians 3:13-14 NIV)

ENDNOTES

1. Interview With Al Roker on The Today Show at **www.shaunrobinson.com**

2. Allyson Byrd as told to by Paula White. "How to Use Blogging, Podcasting, Social Media and Internet Meeting as a Life Coach" interview with Pam Perry. Accessed on April 21, 2011 from **www.blogtalkradio.com/ministrymarketingsolutions**

3. Demetria L. Lucas, *Commentary: The Black Men Shortage.* Posted December 29, 2009 on **www.essence.com/ relationships/commentary_3/black_women_arent_ the_only_ones_looking.php**

4. *Experiments in Living: The Fatherless Family* by Rebecca O'Neill, **www.civitas.org.uk/pubs/experiments.php**

5. From *God Calling*, published by Barbour Publishing, Inc. Used by permission.

acknowledgements

As I wrote this book, sometimes my progress hit a road-block because of self-doubt. I would compare myself to other authors, and look at books on the shelf at my local bookstores, asking myself, "Who would want to read a book about my life and insights? Who cares what I have to say? I'm not rich or famous." A few things I discussed in this book are still issues I have to contend with at times, but with God's leading and inspiration from so many of my friends, church family, my life coach, and my PR coach, today you hold my published book. Wow. God is good all the time!

I have to say thank you to so many people for helping me write this book, which I believe will be the first of many.

To God, the Creator and the Ruler of heaven and earth, for creating me, and giving me the strength to do all that I do. You are my Lord and you are my Friend.

To my family—Mom, Dad, Daj, and Darien. I am fortunate to have no memories without you in them. I would not be me without you, and I love each one of you.

To my author-friends and mentors: Rae Pearson Benn, Edwina Gary, Tomeka Winborne, and Stephanie Hampton

Credle. Your advice helped me avoid pitfalls along with way, and helped me to stay focused on what was important.

To Sharlita Daniel—are you sure we're not related? You are like a sister to me, and my best friend. I love you and will always be grateful for your friendship and support.

To Cheri Bachofer, my life coach. You saw my vision before I really had it fleshed out, and you reminded me to finish this book so you could buy one for your niece! Thank you for challenging me to think outside the box and see the big picture.

To Rob G. Davis, without whom I would not have a title or structure for this book. How did you inspire me so much in one conversation? You encourage me to be me and I appreciate your support.

To Wendy Burley, who previewed a rough draft of this book on her own time. Thank you for your suggestions, encouragement, and support.

To all of my friends, past and present: our relationship helped fuel the woman I am today.

To my editorial team, led by Marla Markman—helping me craft and shape my message so it could shine brightly among the rest. Without your direction it would have taken a few more years to pull everything together.

To my unlikely supporters: Denene Millner, you are such a gracious and talented woman, and I still can't believe the 'friend in my head' is my friend for real! Montrie Rucker Adams, Lisa Nicole Bell, Dr. Kisha Braithwaite Holden—thank you for supporting my work. I'm thrilled to be in your company.

about the author

DAREE ALLEN is a technical writer and motivational speaker. In her spare time, Daree likes reading and writing (yes, for fun!), watching movies, turbo-kickboxing, Zumba, bowling, dancing (especially line dances) and hanging out with friends. She resides in Atlanta, Georgia, with her daughter, Kaia.

Find her online at:
www.DareesInsights.wordpress.com and **www.DareeAllen.com**.

CPSIA information can be obtained
at www.ICGtesting.com
Printed in the USA
BVHW091927200319
543220BV00008B/145/P